THE AI
ADVANTAGE

Management on the Cutting Edge
Paul Michelman, series editor

The AI Advantage: How to Put the Artificial Intelligence Revolution to Work,
Thomas H. Davenport

THE AI ADVANTAGE

How to Put the Artificial Intelligence Revolution to Work

Thomas H. Davenport

The MIT Press
Cambridge, Massachusetts
London, England

First MIT Press paperback edition, 2019

This book was set in Stone Serif by Westchester Publishing Services. Printed and bound in the United States of America.

Library of Congress Cataloging-in-Publication Data

Names: Davenport, Thomas H., 1954- author.
Title: The AI advantage : how to put the artificial intelligence revolution
   to work / Thomas H. Davenport.
Description: Cambridge, MA : MIT Press, [2018] | Series: Management on the
   cutting edge | Includes bibliographical references and index.
Identifiers: LCCN 2018014665 | ISBN 9780262039178 (hardcover : alk. paper),
   9780262538008 (pb.)
Subjects: LCSH: Artificial intelligence--Economic aspects. | Artificial
   intelligence--Industrial applications. | Technological
innovations--Economic aspects.
Classification: LCC HC79.I55 D369 2018 | DDC 658/.0563--dc23 LC record
   available at https://lccn.loc.gov/2018014665

10 9 8 7 6

Contents

Contents

Series Foreword

The world does not lack for management ideas. Thousands of researchers, practitioners, and other experts produce tens of thousands of articles, books, papers, posts, and podcasts each year. But only a scant few promise to truly move the needle on practice, and fewer still dare to reach into the future of what management will become. It is this rare breed of idea—meaningful to practice, grounded in evidence, and *built for the future*—that we seek to present in this series.

Paul Michelman
Editor in chief
MIT Sloan Management Review

Preface

I've been interested in artificial intelligence for a long time. In 1986, for example, I was head of a technology management research center called PRISM (Partnership for Research in Information Systems Management). Working closely with the late MIT professor and business reengineering guru Michael Hammer, we researched a variety of topics that year, but I was particularly excited about one. Called "Expert Systems: Prospects and Early Development," it addressed the fast-growing area of artificial intelligence (AI)—the precursor term for what is often called "cognitive technologies." Expert systems were the AI technology that most excited businesses at the time.

PRISM had fifty or so large corporate sponsors, and many of them had expert system pilots. The technology seemed ready for prime time. All around the Kendall Square neighborhood of Cambridge, Massachusetts, where I worked, the excitement about AI was palpable. My company, Index Systems, was primarily a consulting firm, but we had just spun off a startup, Applied Expert Systems (Apex), to develop an expert system for financial planning. Next door, MIT started the Computer Science and AI Lab (CSAIL), which continues today. Just down the street from my office was the headquarters of Symbolics, the leading company that built dedicated Lisp (a programming language well suited to AI applications) machines. As something of an aside, I remember reading on March 15, 1985, that Symbolics had just registered the first internet domain name— Symbolics.com.

Over the decades I remained interested in the technologies and how companies were using them. During the 1990s and early 2000s I was primarily working on knowledge management and analytics (starting in the late 1990s), and AI was in one of its several "winters" of low commercial enthusiasm. However, I was still very interested in how AI was being used in business. Rule engines were still the dominant technology in that era, and some companies—including Accenture, where I ran a research center—were making money from building and using them. My then-Accenture colleague Jeanne Harris and I set out to study them. Our resulting 2005 article "Automated Decision Making Comes of Age" described the companies, many of them in the financial services industry, that were getting substantial value from the technology. But this article didn't lead to a winter snap; of all my publications, according to Google Scholar it is the eighty-sixth most often cited, with only ninety-nine brave souls mentioning it in print!

Since most of my work over the past decade or two involves analytics and big data, I tried to follow that movement wherever it led. And over the past two or three years it has been clear that it is leading to AI. I'll argue throughout this book that AI is a largely analytical technology, and that for most organizations working with it AI is a straightforward extension of what they do with data and analytics.

I would normally have written this book on enterprise uses of AI/cognitive a couple of years ago. The enterprise is usually my focus when a new set of technologies emerges; I wrote books on that with enterprise resource planning (ERP) systems, knowledge management, analytics, and big data. But a couple of years ago there weren't very many large enterprises that were making effective use of this technology. I wrote another book (with Julia Kirby) on what AI means for workers and their jobs, and by the time that one came out in 2016, enterprises were increasingly jumping on the bandwagon. The world is clearly ready for a book that charts the path of artificial intelligence and cognitive technologies in mainstream businesses. What follows is my attempt at such a book.

Acknowledgments

There are five classes of people I'd like to thank for their help with this book: my family, my agent, my publisher, my consulting partners, and my sources of insight. At the beginning of the process came my agent Rafe Sagalyn, who has represented me on three books now. He did a huge amount more than just finding me a publisher—although he did that very well. Rafe read numerous drafts of the proposal and helped me define much more clearly what I wanted to write about. And I believe the title was his idea too. I have been lucky to work with him multiple times.

This was my first book with the MIT Press, and I had a great experience. Emily Taber was both pleasant and insightful to work with, and she did an excellent job of editing the manuscript with just the right touch. And I really appreciated her tinkering with the external review process to speed it up a bit. Michael Sims proved a great copy editor, which is probably why he is the managing editor of the Press. And I was very happy to collaborate with Paul Michelman, an old friend who's now editor in chief at *MIT Sloan Management Review*, to write the first book in *SMR*'s collaboration with the Press.

I say this in almost every book, but you may not have read them: I make my living by writing about the heroic achievements of practicing managers. This book is no exception. Thanks to all those people in companies who spoke with me and let me write about their successes and their challenges with artificial intelligence. More on them inside. I also got help from practitioners at vendors and services firms, including Vikram Mahidhar at Genpact, Manoj Saxena and Akshay Sabhikhi at Cognitive Scale, Barry Liebert at OpenMatters, and various folks at Salesforce.com, SAS, SAP, IBM, Tamr, and LoopAI Labs.

I've been a senior advisor to Deloitte for eight years now, and this book shows the fruits of that relationship more than any other I've written. I learned a lot about AI in enterprises from two Deloitte efforts in which I participated: a survey of executives familiar with AI use in their companies, and an analysis of 152 consulting projects on AI. For the Deloitte collaborations I would like to thank Alyssa Pharr, Paul Roma (now at Ciox Health), Rajeev Ronanki, David Schatsky, Jeff Loucks, Christina Scoby, Kerry Iseman, Ryan Renner, Nitin Mittal, Dave Rudini, Greg Szwartz, Giovanni Faccioli, and many others at the firm who provided help along the way.

My family has always been supportive of my compelling need to bang away for hours on the keyboard. Mostly I want to thank my wife of several decades, Jodi. In addition to providing massive emotional support, she also offered many great ideas about the subject, the title, the publication process, and so forth. Thanks, Sweetie. And thanks to all my extended family members (Hayes, Chase, Geneva, Kim, Bob, Helen, Alex, Lawson) who always express interest in yet another book—it can't be easy!

1 Artificial Intelligence Comes of Age—Slowly

Perhaps it was the success of IBM's Watson in beating—actually, decimating—the best human players of the television game *Jeopardy!* in January 2011 that encouraged other organizations to take on highly ambitious "moon shots" with artificial intelligence (AI). After they saw an AI system dominate a game show with difficult and oddly worded questions and answers, people may have begun to believe that AI could take on any problem—even curing cancer.

In March 2012 IBM agreed with Memorial Sloan Kettering Cancer Center in New York to jointly develop the Watson Oncology Advisor to help physicians diagnose and treat cancer. The hospital was somewhat reserved about the collaboration; a press release at the time promised no miracles:

Memorial Sloan Kettering Cancer Center and IBM announced the formation of a collaboration to develop a powerful cancer resource, built on the IBM Watson system, to provide medical professionals with improved access to current and comprehensive cancer data and practices. The new decision-support tool will help physicians everywhere create individualized cancer diagnostic and treatment recommendations for their patients.[1]

Not to be outdone by its traditional rival, M.D. Anderson Cancer Center in Houston announced in October 2013 that it had contracted with IBM a year earlier to assist in the development of the Oncology Expert Advisor (OEA), with Watson as the underlying technology. The project was designated one of M.D. Anderson's Moon Shot Program projects, with strong support from the hospital's CEO.

Only a month after the project was announced, an M.D. Anderson blog post suggested that the project to address cancer—leukemia in particular—was virtually solved. It contained an interview with a leukemia researcher at the hospital, who commented:

The OEA enables us to provide better, more personalized care through accurate and evidence-based treatment recommendations based upon a specific patient's characteristics as well as his or her leukemia-specific characteristics. The OEA also can help doctors identify the best cancer treatment for a particular patient by identifying both the standard treatment options and clinical trials for which a patient is eligible.... Additionally, by following a patient over time along with the physician, the OEA helps minimize potential adverse events and optimize management of the patient's care at all times.[2]

M.D. Anderson received a $50 million donation from an Asian billionaire to pay for the project, and hired a consultant to help implement the system. Progress wasn't immediate, and press accounts with quotes from M.D. Anderson personnel equated the project as "sending Watson to med school." One worrisome story in the *Wall Street Journal* quoted the head of the Watson business unit at the time as saying that the M.D. Anderson project was "in a ditch" in 2013.[3] But other press accounts remained positive, like this article in the *Washington Post:*

Candida Vitale and the other fellows at MD Anderson's leukemia treatment center had known one another for only a few months, but they already were very tight. The nine of them shared a small office and were always hanging out on weekends.... But she wasn't quite sure what to make of the new guy, ...Rumor had it that he had finished med school in two years and had a photographic memory of thousands of journal articles and relevant clinical trials. When the fellows were asked to summarize patients' records for the senior faculty in the mornings, he always seemed to have the best answers.... "I was surprised," said Vitale, a 31-year-old who received her MD in Italy. "Even if you work all night, it would be impossible to be able to put this much information together like that." ...The new guy's name was a mouthful, so many of his colleagues simply called him by his nickname: Watson.[4]

In November of 2016, however, the University of Texas System (of which M.D. Anderson is a part) Audit Office revealed that the Houston-based hospital had a problem. It released a bombshell report: "Special Review of Procurement Procedures Related to the M.D. Anderson Cancer Center Oncology Expert Advisor Project." The audit reported that the OEA had cost $62 million thus far, that it had not been used to treat a single patient, that it was not at all integrated with the hospital's electronic medical record system, and that poor project management and accounting approaches had been used on the project. The OEA project was put on indefinite hold; in effect, Watson had taken a leave from med school without ever seeing a sick patient. The project leader had already left for another job in the UT System in 2015. A few months after the auditor's report, the CEO submitted his resignation.

Throughout much of the time the OEA project was underway, however, in another corner of M.D. Anderson other AI projects were also being pursued. Under the leadership of Chief Information Officer Chris Belmont (whose IT organization, as the audit report pointed out, was not substantially involved in the OEA project), these AI initiatives were much less ambitious and expensive. They included a "care concierge" that makes hotel and restaurant recommendations for patients' families, an application to determine which patients most needed help paying bills, and an automated "cognitive help desk" for addressing staff IT problems. The recommendations are being integrated into the hospital's patient portal, and a variety of new cognitive projects are being developed. The new systems have contributed to an increase in patient satisfaction and financial performance at the hospital, and a decline in tedious data entry by the hospital's care managers. Despite the setback on the cancer treatment moon shot, M.D. Anderson is committed to cognitive technology and is developing a center of competency to address it.

M.D. Anderson also hasn't given up on the use of AI for cancer diagnosis and treatment. Another moon shot program is called APOLLO (Adaptive Patient-Oriented Longitudinal Learning and Optimization), and uses machine learning to generate detailed predictive models of how patients with different genomic profiles and medical histories respond to cancer treatments.[5] Although the project uses (or suffers from) similar ambitious space terminology used to describe the Oncology Expert Advisor, it relies on machine learning methods that have been well established for decades, and is similar to projects taking place at a number of other cancer research centers.

DBS Bank, based in Singapore, is the largest bank in Southeast Asia and is a leader in using technology to enhance service and operations.

Its name was once satirized as meaning "damn bloody slow," but DBS was named the best digital bank in the world by *Euromoney* magazine in 2016. AI has been a focus of the bank for several years. It was one of the earliest commercial organizations to contract with IBM to develop an AI application. The goal of the application, announced in January 2014, was to produce an intelligent "robo-advisor" that would advise DBS clients on wealth management and investment opportunities. Other financial institutions have robo-advisors, but they tend to lack a high degree of intelligence in their recommendations.

DBS wanted a system that could digest a variety of inputs—research reports, company news, indicators of market sentiment, and the customer's existing portfolio—and then make recommendations to the bank's relationship managers and their customers. But David Gledhill, the chief information officer of DBS, commented that the technology wasn't quite ready for this ambitious problem:

We were very early on, and at the time the Watson technology wasn't that mature. It wasn't production-ready to be the well-rounded next-generation wealth advisor that that both DBS and IBM planned for it to be: We were way ahead of the curve when we embarked on this project. In hindsight, the technology was not mature enough. It wasn't production-ready for many of our use cases. Part of the problem was that the software wasn't able to make sense of the myriad of charts and graphs that we needed it to. Furthermore, the bank's research reports also came in many different formats, making it difficult for Watson to analyze the data without a lot of human intervention. So while we developed a robo-advisor pilot, it wasn't half as effective or productive as the average relationship manager. And so, we took the learnings and stopped the project pretty early in the cycle.

Gledhill and his colleagues continue to assess new technologies that might be capable of addressing the intelligent robo-advisor use case, although they haven't found anything yet. But their faith in the value of AI is undiminished. They have focused their attention on important but somewhat less ambitious problems in their business for which cognitive technologies can provide significant improvements.

The AI projects that DBS has undertaken cover a wide variety of areas, but most address operational processes. For example, the bank uses machine learning models to predict when ATM machines need to be refilled with cash. Instead of running out once every three months on average, the average is now once in fifty-five years, and replenishment trips have been reduced by over 10 percent.

In human resources, DBS is predicting churn of its salespeople. Using factors like timing of holidays and medical leaves taken, and even how quickly employees answer emails—factors identified with machine learning models—it can now predict with 85 percent accuracy whether someone will leave within three months.

The bank is also using AI to detect fraud in trading, for algorithm-based lending models, for chatbots in customer service, and several other uses. AI plays a particularly large role in DBS's "digibank" in India—a digital-only bank with 90 percent fewer people than a traditional bank. Throughout the entire bank, AI-based customer interactions are reducing the volume of calls made to the call center by 15 percent.

Gledhill commented on the change in AI focus for DBS:

> The initial robo-advisor was our most ambitious project, and it didn't go as planned because we were expecting something way ahead of our time. But we learned from that first project and didn't back away from AI at all. We are "picking low hanging fruit" by using AI to optimize business processes across the bank and are seeing huge amounts of success with it. These projects are less ambitious individually, but are transformative in their aggregate as they contribute to lowering operating expenses, increasing employee productivity, reducing error rates, and increasing speed-to-market. Our primary goal is not to reduce headcount, but to create a much better experience for the customer, and go beyond transactional banking to relationship banking. We are looking to grow our revenue and our business while maintaining a reasonable cost-income ratio.

The most aggressive users of artificial intelligence—both in their products and their internal processes—have been tech companies like Amazon.com. That fast-growing firm claims that it has been "investing deeply" in AI for over twenty years—almost its entire history.[6] AI and machine learning technologies are at the core of Amazon's successful voice recognition products, Echo/Alexa. And Amazon has some highly visible and potentially transformational applications of AI in its business model, including its delivery by drones project Prime Air, and fully automated checkout at Amazon Go convenience stores.

These projects face significant technical, behavioral, and regulatory challenges, and are not fully launched. However, Amazon seems likely to at least partially accomplish some of these moon shots (I recently visited the Amazon Go store in Seattle, and the automated checkout system seems to work quite well—although the store still has several employees). Few companies would seem to have more capabilities than Amazon to pull them off. The company has many AI algorithms—both open source and proprietary—that it offers to customers, and uses itself, on Amazon Web Services. No one seems to know exactly how many data scientists work at the company, but at the moment 505 job openings can be found in that category at Amazon. The company's own recruiting website lists 171 open jobs in artificial intelligence. Both numbers are far more than most companies employ or could even imagine hiring.[7] If anyone could create ambitious, complex, and highly visible cognitive technologies for internal and external use, it would seem to be this organization.

However, in his 2017 letter to shareholders of Amazon.com, Jeff Bezos argued that the primary impact of AI (or machine learning in particular) at the company would be important but invisible:

But much of what we do with machine learning happens beneath the surface. Machine learning drives our algorithms for demand forecasting, product search ranking, product and deals recommendations, merchandising placements, fraud detection, translations, and much more. Though less visible, much of the impact of machine learning will be of this type—quietly but meaningfully improving core operations.[8]

Get Cognitive Slow

Despite several decades of "AI winters" and "AI springs" where research into AI fell out of favor and was then revitalized, AI is all the rage today. Large organizations like M.D. Anderson, DBS, and Amazon are embracing it. Tech startups in Silicon Valley and elsewhere, and professional services firms all see AI as the next—or even the current—big thing. Venture capital firms are pouring money into the field. Media attention and hype is higher than ever for the technology.

I certainly agree that some of this excitement is warranted. When AI technology is up to the task, and when the problem isn't exceedingly difficult and complex—like curing cancer, capturing all of a large bank's knowledge about investing, or managing a fleet of drones without human pilots—it can succeed and yield significant benefits. But artificial intelligence isn't going to transform the work of organizations—or the lives of individuals—as fast as many people seem to expect. It will be one of the many technologies that comply with Amara's Law (named after the scientist and futurist Roy Amara):

We tend to overestimate the effect of a technology in the short run and under-estimate the effect in the long run.[9]

In the short run, AI will provide evolutionary benefits; in the long run, it is likely to be revolutionary.

AI does offer a lot of business value, but much of that value isn't terribly sexy or visible. Products and processes will be made somewhat better and easier to use. Decisions will be better informed. We'll continue—and perhaps even accelerate a bit—the amazing progress that we've seen over the last couple of decades in data and analytics. But as all of the early adopters have discovered, it's still difficult to create systems that think and communicate like humans—even in narrow domains. This is particularly true with AI technologies that are relatively new and complex, as IBM Watson was when M.D. Anderson and DBS tried to apply it.

While there are clearly many sources of potential business value from AI, there is a valid question of just how visible AI and its benefits will be in organizations. The technology could lead to dramatic transformation in a series of moon shots, or it could be important but largely invisible. I think the latter future is somewhat more likely. Remember that real moon shots were preceded by a number of less ambitious space flights. Back in 2014, the technology prognosticator Kevin Kelly wrote that the AI he foresees is more like a kind of "cheap, reliable, industrial-grade digital smartness running behind everything, and almost invisible except when it blinks off." Kelly compared AI to electricity, arguing that, "There is almost nothing we can think of that cannot be made new, different, or interesting by infusing it with some extra IQ. ... Like all utilities, AI will be supremely boring, even as it transforms the Internet, the global economy, and civilization."[10]

As at Amazon, there may be opportunities for capable organizations to develop prominent and highly ambitious applications. But they are likely to be few and far between, and the chances of them missing the moon are relatively high. However, more prosaic opportunities are plenty valuable to make cognitive technologies worth pursuing.

There should be no doubt that AI is worth the attention of businesses, but they need to experiment with the technology and build enough experience to use it effectively. Some early projects have already failed or encountered substantial difficulties because neither the technologies nor the organizations using them were quite ready. Just as the smartest investors "get rich slow," companies will need to become more cognitive slowly over time. The businesses and organizations that succeed with AI will be those that invest steadily, rise above the hype, make a good match between their business problems and the capabilities of AI, and take the long view. This book describes how companies can take that approach.

However, I'll also argue that it is dangerous to do nothing in this area, or to move too slowly. I speak with large, established firms almost every day that have realized the power of this technology. Later on I'll mention substantial majorities of surveyed managers in these established firms who believe that cognitive technologies will transform both their internal processes and their products and services. Those companies and managers are likely to be your competitors, and it would be foolish not to begin building AI capabilities today.

The other major threat, of course, is disruptive startups. As I've already suggested, the most aggressive adopters of AI have been online "digital native" firms like Google, Amazon, and Facebook. We've already seen how these data-driven firms have entered a variety of industries and challenged established leaders. Google, for example, has used its extensive mapping data and its prowess at AI to become a strong competitor in the autonomous vehicle industry.

We're also likely to see numerous startups in particular industry sectors that focus on AI as a core component of their business models. Take, for example, the property and casualty (P&C) insurance industry, with many established U.S. firms like State Farm, Allstate, Geico,

Progressive, and others. Some of those firms, like Progressive, were strong in traditional data analytics, but it's not clear that any of them has taken a very aggressive approach to incorporating AI into their businesses.

But those established firms are being disrupted by startups like Lemonade, a New York–based startup that has put AI at the center of its business. As its CEO and cofounder Daniel Schreiber wrote in a blog post:

In recent years the insurance industry has paid close attention to insurance-tech-startups. They take note of how being digital transforms the user experience, appeals to younger consumers, and removes costs, while expediting everything. That's all true, but it is only Act 1. ... While everyone is bedazzled by the tech of Act 1, these delightful apps are generating mountains of data. These will soon reach the billions of entries that machines go to town on, and that's when Act 2 will begin. ... Act 1 showcases the power of technology to transform *any* business by reducing costs, increasing speed, and delighting consumers. But when Act 2 begins, we will see the power of AI to transform insurance in a *uniquely* powerful way. It will go beyond thrilling customers and driving efficiencies, to being able to quantify risk like never before. That day is nigh.[11]

Of course, established firms in P&C insurance are responding to this competitive threat. Sompo Holdings, a large insurance firm based in Japan (where I am an advisor), is pursuing AI across multiple fronts (although startups like Lemonade are currently less of a threat in Japan). It was an early experimenter with IBM Watson's intelligent agent application for customer service. It is generating predictive models with automated machine learning. It is using AI to extract key data from requests for business insurance, and modeling weather data with machine learning. Sompo's CEO, Kengo Sakurada, and its chief digital officer, Koichi Narasaki, are well aware of the power of AI to change their business and are determined to explore the technology aggressively.

What Do We Mean by AI/Cognitive Technologies?

Broadly speaking, AI or cognitive technologies employ such capabilities—previously possessed only by humans—as knowledge, insight, and perception to solve narrowly defined (with the current state of technology) tasks. The tasks are those that can usually be accomplished quickly by humans—identifying an image or interpreting the meaning of a sentence. Befitting the "cognitive" label, these tasks could once be performed only by human brains. Few today would debate this high-level definition, although there is certainly debate about how close AI comes to duplicating brain structures and functions (my view is not very close thus far).

It's important to realize, however, that there is considerable ambiguity in the day-to-day application of the terms *artificial intelligence* or *cognitive technologies*. Some observers include highly statistical approaches like machine learning, even though machine learning often has more to do with traditional analytics than with other forms of AI. Some who do think of machine learning as artificially intelligent even prefer it as a general term over AI. Some include in AI robotic process automation (RPA) technology, which at least up to now hasn't been terribly intelligent. I will take a relatively inclusive approach to the topic, in part because the world seems to want a broad interpretation of the AI term, and also because all of the candidate technologies are becoming more intelligent over time.

As this discussion suggests, another complicating factor in the enterprise use of AI is that there are several different underlying technologies that comprise the topic. And for most of the technologies, there are several alternative functions they can perform. The combinations of technologies and functions are sufficiently complex that one AI researcher, Kris Hammond, has proposed a "periodic table" of AI.[12] Below is a table of seven key technologies, a brief description of each, and some typical functions or applications they can perform.

I will also describe how common each technology is in the world of business AI. I work with many different companies and am primarily a business school professor, but I am also a senior advisor to Deloitte's strategy and analytics practice, which incorporates consulting work in AI. In that role I helped to develop and analyze a 2017 survey of 250 senior "cognitive aware" managers in the United States—those whose organizations are actively using the technology and who understand its application and use. One of the questions asked what technologies were being used at the respondents' companies.

Below the table is a deeper description of each technology and its functionality.

Technology	Brief Description	Example Applications
Statistical machine learning	Automates process of training and fitting models to data	Highly granular marketing analyses on big data
Neural networks	Uses artificial "neurons" to weight inputs and relate them to outputs	Identifying credit fraud, weather prediction
Deep learning	Neural networks with many layers of variables or features	Image and voice recognition, extracting meaning from text
Natural language processing	Analyzes and "understands" human speech and text	Speech recognition, chatbots, intelligent agents
Rule-based expert systems	A set of logical rules derived from human experts	Insurance underwriting, credit approval
Physical robots	Automates a physical activity	Factory and warehouse tasks
Robotic process automation	Automates structured digital tasks and interfaces with systems	Credit card replacement, validating online credentials

Statistical Machine Learning

Machine learning is a technique for automatically fitting models to data and to "learn" by training models with data. Machine learning is one of the most common forms of AI; in a 2017 Deloitte survey of 250 "cognitive aware" managers whose organizations were already pursuing AI, 58 percent of companies surveyed were employing machine learning in their businesses. It is a broad technique at the core of many approaches to artificial intelligence, and there are many versions of it. The explosion of data within and outside firms—and particularly these external data—has made it both feasible and necessary for them to adopt machine learning to make sense of it all.

A more complex form of machine learning is the *neural network*—a technology that has been available since the 1960s and has been used for categorization applications like determining whether a credit transaction is fraudulent. It views problems in terms of inputs, outputs, and weights of variables or "features" that associate inputs with outputs. It has been likened to the way that neurons process signals, but the analogy to the brain isn't a strong one.

The most complex forms of machine learning involve *deep learning*, or neural network models with many levels of features or variables that predict outcomes. There may be thousands of features in such models, which is enabled by the faster processing of today's computer architectures. Unlike earlier forms of statistical analysis, each feature in a deep learning model typically has little meaning to a human observer. As a result the models are very difficult or impossible to interpret. In the Deloitte survey, 34 percent were using deep learning technologies.

Deep learning models use a technique called *backpropogation* to make the models predict or classify outputs.[13] Deep learning using backpropogation is the AI technology that has been responsible for many of the most recent advances in the field, from beating human experts at the game of Go to classifying images on the internet. Geoffrey Hinton of the University of Toronto and Google is often called the father of deep learning, in part because of his early work on backpropogation.

Machine learning employs more than a hundred possible algorithms, most of them somewhat esoteric. They range from *gradient boosting* (an approach that builds models that addresses errors of previous models, thus boosting the predictive or classification ability) to *random forests* (models that are collections of decision tree models). Increasingly software tools (including DataRobot, SAS, and Google's AutoML) allow the automated construction of machine learning models that tries out many different algorithms to see which is most successful.[14] Once the best model is found to predict or classify the training data, it is deployed to predict or classify new data—sometimes called a scoring process.

In addition to the algorithm used, another key dimension of machine learning is how the models learn. Supervised learning models (by far the most common type used in business) learn from a set of training data with a labeled outcome. For example, a machine learning model attempting to predict fraud in a bank would need to be trained on a system in which fraud has been clearly established in some cases. This isn't easy to do, because the frequency of actual fraud might be only 1 in 100,000 cases—sometimes referred to as a *class imbalance*.

Supervised learning is very similar to a traditional analytical method like regression analysis that is deployed in a scoring model. In regression analysis, the objective is to create a model to predict a known outcome using a set of input variables with known values that might be associated with that outcome. Once a model has been developed, it can be used with known values of the same input variables to predict an unknown outcome. For example, we might develop a regression model to predict the likelihood of contracting diabetes given a patient's age, physical activity level, caloric consumption, and body mass index. We develop the model on patients whom we already know did develop diabetes or did not—normally using all the available data to develop the regression model. Once we have found a good predictive regression model, we can use it in a new set of data to predict an unknown outcome—the likelihood that a patient will develop diabetes given certain levels of the input variables. This latter activity (in both regression analysis and machine learning) is called *scoring*.

This regression process is the same as supervised machine learning except that:

• In machine learning, the data used for the development (training) of the model are called *training data*, and may be a subset of the data held out explicitly for training purposes;

• In machine learning, the training model is often validated using another subset of the data for which the outcome to be predicted is known;

• In regression, there may not be a desire to use a model to predict unknown outcomes, whereas that is assumed in machine learning;

• Many different algorithm types may be used in machine learning instead of just simple regression analysis.

Unsupervised models, which are usually more difficult to develop, detect patterns in data that aren't labeled and for which the result isn't known. A third variation, *reinforcement learning*, is when machine learning systems have a defined goal and each move toward it yields a form of reward. It has been very useful in playing games, but also requires a lot of data—in many cases, too much data for the method to be useful.[15] It's important to point out that supervised machine learning models don't generally learn continuously; they learn from a set of training data, and then they continue to use the same model unless a new set of training data is employed to teach new models.

Machine learning models are based on statistics, and they should be compared to conventional analytics to establish their incremental value. They tend to be more accurate than traditional "artisanal" analytical models based on human hypotheses and regression analysis, but more complex and difficult to interpret. Automated machine learning models can be created much more quickly and can describe more detailed datasets than traditional statistical analysis. Given the requisite amount of data from which to learn, deep learning models are very good at tasks like image and voice recognition—far better than earlier automated approaches to these tasks, and approaching or exceeding human capabilities in some areas.

Natural Language Processing (NLP)

Making sense of human language has been a goal of AI researchers since the 1950s. This field, called *natural language processing*, includes applications such as speech recognition, text analysis, translation, generation, and other goals related to language. Fifty-three percent of companies in the "cognitive aware" survey were using NLP. There are two basic approaches to it: statistical vs. semantic NLP. Statistical NLP is based on machine learning and appears to be improving its capabilities faster than semantic NLP. It requires a large "corpus" or body of language from which to learn. In translation, for example, it requires a large body of translated texts and through statistical analysis comes to learn that *amor* in Spanish and Portuguese is highly correlated statistically with the word *love* in English. It's a "brute force" but often quite effective approach.

Semantic NLP was the only real option pursued until the past decade or so, and it can be moderately effective if words, syntax, and concept relationships are trained into the system effectively. The training and *knowledge engineering* of language—often referred to as creating a *knowledge graph* within a particular domain—can be labor-intensive and time-consuming, however. It requires the development of ontologies, or models of the relationships between words and phrases. Although it is difficult to create semantic NLP models, several intelligent agent systems make use of that approach today.

The performance of NLP systems should be measured in two ways. One is the percentage of spoken words of which it can make sense. That metric is increasing with deep learning technology and is often above 95 percent. The other way to measure NLP is how many different types of questions it can answer or issues it can address. That typically requires semantic NLP, and since there is no big technical breakthrough in that area, question-answering or issue-resolving systems are context specific and must be trained. IBM Watson did a great job of answering *Jeopardy!* questions, but it can't answer *Wheel of Fortune* questions unless it is trained—often in a labor-intensive fashion. Perhaps in the future deep learning will be applied to question answering, but it hasn't been yet.

Rule-Based Expert Systems

Expert systems based on collections of if-then rules were the dominant technology for AI in the 1980s, and were widely used commercially in that and later periods. Today they aren't generally considered to be state-of-the-art, but according to the 2017 Deloitte "cognitive aware" survey, 49 percent of U.S. companies that work with AI are still using them.

Expert systems require human experts and knowledge engineers to construct a series of rules in a particular knowledge domain. They have been commonly employed, for example, in insurance underwriting and bank credit underwriting—but also in esoteric domains like coffee roasting at Folgers, or soup cooking at Campbell's. They work well up to a point, and are easy to understand. However, when the number of rules is large (usually over several hundred) and the rules begin to conflict with each other, they tend to break down. And if the knowledge domain changes, changing the rules can be difficult and time-consuming.

Rule-based systems haven't improved much since their earlier heyday, but industries like insurance and banking that make a lot of use of them are hoping for a new generation of rule-based technology to come along. Researchers and vendors are beginning to discuss "adaptive rule engines" that would modify rules continuously based on new data, or combinations of rule engines and machine learning—but they are certainly not yet in wide use.

Physical Robots

Physical robots are well known by this point, given that more than 200,000 industrial robots are installed each year around the world. Thirty-two percent of companies in the U.S. "cognitive aware" survey were using physical robots in some capacity. They perform tasks like lifting, repositioning, welding, or assembling objects in places like factories and warehouses. They have historically been guided by detailed computer programs that allowed them to do particular tasks. More recently, however, robots have become more collaborative with humans and are more easily trained by moving them through a desired task. They are also becoming more intelligent, as other AI capabilities are being embedded in their "brains" (really their operating systems). Over time it seems likely that the same improvements in intelligence that we've seen in other areas of AI would be incorporated into physical robots.

Robotic Process Automation (RPA)

This technology performs structured digital tasks—that is, those involving information systems—as if they were a human user following a script or rules. There is justifiable debate about whether RPA belongs in a collection of AI/cognitive technologies, because it's not terribly smart. But because RPA systems are popular, automated, and getting smarter, I include them in the AI world. Some refer to them as "digital labor," and compared to other forms of AI they are inexpensive, easy to program, and transparent in their actions. If you can point and click, understand graphical models of process flows, and identify some if/then business rules, you can understand and perhaps even develop RPA. These systems are also much easier to configure and implement than alternative approaches like developing your own programs in a programming language.

RPA doesn't really involve robots—only computer programs on servers. It relies on a combination of workflow, business rules, and "presentation layer" integration with information systems to act like a semi-intelligent user of the systems. Some compare RPA to spreadsheet macros, but I don't think this is a fair comparison; RPA can perform substantially more complex tasks. It is also compared to business process management (BPM) tools, which may have some workflow capabilities but are generally designed to document and analyze a business process, not actually automate it.[16]

Some RPA systems already have a degree of intelligence. They can "observe" human colleagues doing their work—answering frequent customer questions, for example—and then emulate their actions. Others can combine process automation with machine vision. Like physical robots, RPA systems are slowly becoming more intelligent, and other types of AI technologies are being used to guide their behavior.

I've described these technologies as individual ones, but increasingly they are being combined and integrated. For the moment, however, it's very important for a business decision maker to know something about what technologies do what kinds of tasks. Krishna Nathan, CIO of Global Inc., notes that one of his key priorities in 2018 is "helping my stakeholders understand what AI can and cannot do so we can use it in the right ways."[17] Perhaps in the future these technologies will be so intermingled that such an understanding won't be as necessary or even feasible.

AI in the Vendor Community

My focus in this book is the use of cognitive technologies by large enterprises in businesses like financial services, manufacturing, and telecommunications. But much of the work being undertaken by large commercial enterprises has been made possible by research and product development at many of the same places where big data technologies (such as Hadoop, Pig, and Hive) had been developed in the 2000s. Google, Facebook, and to a lesser degree Yahoo all had substantial AI efforts underway in this period. These companies had massive amounts of data to analyze, enormous amounts of money to spend (at least in the case of Google and Facebook), and great connections with academic researchers.

Google

Google has been, perhaps not surprisingly, the most active developer and user of AI among the Internet giants—and perhaps all companies in the world. The company, working with Stanford professor Andrew Ng, began to research AI (deep learning in particular) in its Google X research labs in 2011. The project came to be known as Google Brain. The method of choice was deep learning, which was used for image recognition, among other tasks. By 2012 the group had conquered one of the most pressing problems of humankind: how to get a machine to identify a photo of a cat on the internet.

The next year, Google hired Geoffrey Hinton, the University of Toronto researcher who had helped to revive neural networks. In 2014 Google bought DeepMind, a London-based firm with deep expertise in deep learning. The group's tools were used to help AlphaGo, Google's machine that plays the ancient game Go, beat one of the world's best human players. In 2016, the Google Brain organization helped Google make a major improvement in the ability of Google Translate to do accurate translations. By that year Google, or its parent company Alphabet, was employing machine learning in over 2,700 different projects across the company, including search algorithms (RankBrain), self-driving cars (now in the Alphabet subsidiary Waymo), and medical diagnostics (in the Calico subsidiary).[18] In the Silicon Valley tradition, Google also made its TensorFlow machine learning library available for free in 2015 as an open source project, and it has become popular among more sophisticated companies that use AI.

Facebook

Facebook may not have been quite as successful as Google in incorporating cognitive technologies into its products and processes, but it has done pretty well. Their equivalent of smart guys Andrew Ng and Geoff Hinton is Yann Lecun, who heads the company's AI research and doubles as an NYU professor. Lecun focuses particularly on image recognition, and that's been a key area of focus for Facebook. The company has an image recognition application called Lumos that analyzes photos on Facebook or Instagram, and offers the user personalized ads on the basis of their content. Lumos also helps to identify banned pornographic or violent content (although numerous humans are still involved in this activity as well), improper use of brands and logos, or terrorism-related content.

But as I'll discuss in detail in chapter 7, Facebook has struggled with some forms of cognitive technology. It has attempted to use it to identify important and relevant news items to present to customers (Facebook Trending Topics), but the automated process found it difficult to distinguish real from fake news. More recently, Russian hackers were able to place deliberately false news on Facebook without detection by automated filters. Automated ad targeting at Facebook has also been blamed for ads targeting racists.[19] In all three cases, Facebook has had to add additional human reviewers. There is hope, however, that cognitive tools can help humans work faster and more effectively to filter fake news or hate speech.[20]

IBM's Watson

IBM, of course, is not generally viewed as a big data and internet giant. But it is the other main company that has advanced cognitive technologies (it generally refers to "cognitive computing") in the marketplace with its Watson offerings. Watson began, of course, as an all-out (and hugely successful) effort to beat human experts at the *Jeopardy!* TV game in 2011. Consistent with that game's format, Watson began as a question-answering system that draws primarily from online textual knowledge.

Now, however, Watson has evolved into a brand rather than a specific capability. The brand encompasses offerings related not only to cognitive question answering, but also image recognition, weather data analysis, the Internet of Things, and basic statistical analysis and reporting. Even "cognitive Watson" involves a set of application program interfaces (APIs)—small, modular programs that take in data, perform a specific task, and send back a result—that can be mixed and integrated to address specific problems.

The good news about Watson is that it is a capable "platform" for cognitive technology work—one of the few available. By most accounts its APIs work as promised. And the company has done a yeoman's work in creating the "Watson ecosystem" of smaller companies that use some Watson capabilities in their own offerings.

But there is also bad news about Watson, and many in the AI community have come to view it negatively.[21] The company's marketing has gotten ahead of its ability to deliver results. IBM claims, for example, to have already mastered the treatment of six types of cancer, but the actual results as evaluated by cancer-oriented researchers and institutions are far more equivocal.[22] No objective, rigorous research articles have evaluated its healthcare projects. And in healthcare and other industries, when Watson does deliver results, it's usually only with the aid of large numbers of IBM's (or other firms') consultants. Watson was criticized for this in a 2017 investor analysis report by Jeffries & Co.[23]

In short, IBM is both hero and villain in the latest round of enthusiasm about cognitive technologies. No doubt its impressive *Jeopardy!* win and the marketing thereof contributed greatly to the current level of enthusiasm about the technologies. But if there is another "AI winter" anytime soon from the failure of cognitive technologies to meet over-hyped expectations, IBM will deserve a big chunk of the blame. More judicious marketing—and more exposure to what the system can actually do, and can't—would help to prevent that fate.

What's Coming in This Book

The goal of this chapter was to introduce you to cognitive technology and to begin to address the overall context for its use by large organizations and vendors. Although the most dramatic use of cognitive technologies has been within vendor firms and we can learn a lot from them, we can't forget that the purpose of their activity is to enable capabilities within "user" enterprises. And that happens to be the focus of this book. To my mind, the issues of embedding smart machines into their products, services, strategies, cultures, and behaviors are the most interesting problems with AI. Chapter 2, then, addresses head-on some of the opportunities and challenges involved in AI within the enterprise.

In chapter 3, I'll describe in greater detail what technologies, applications, and benefits companies are pursuing, and the types of AI capabilities they are attempting to build.

In chapter 4, I'll argue the virtues of a strategy for cognitive technology. It's hard to ensure that your investments and explorations will have an impact without one, or at least without answering some strategic questions. I'll say a bit about the process for developing one, and then go into detail about the topics that it should address.

Chapters 5 through 7 explore several emerging aspects of organizations that make effective use of cognitive technology. Chapter 5 discusses the changes in organizational structures and business processes that cognitive technology can bring with automation and knowledge support for key tasks. Chapter 6 is devoted to new roles and skills that will be required of workers in cognitive companies. And chapter 7 describes changes in technologies and data that need to be present before an organization can succeed. Many of the lessons in these three chapters apply not only to those who use cognitive technology, but also to those who create it.

The final chapter, chapter 8, addresses issues involving organizational and social changes from AI. It will raise some of the ethical concerns around cognitive technologies that relate specifically to established firms. The chapter will also suggest aspects of how the cognitive company of the future will look and act.

Throughout this book, I have tried to minimize the level of hype—there is plenty of that in the world already—and focus on what's really happening with AI in organizations. If you wanted breathless prose about how AI will change the world tomorrow, you have probably come to the wrong place. If you prefer an honest and straightforward look at the impact this powerful technology will have on businesses over the short and long term, keep reading.

2   AI in the Enterprise

With all the media and vendor hype, you may be concerned that the AI bubble will burst before most organizations can even get started with it. That is what happened the last time there was substantial hype about AI, but I believe another AI winter is relatively unlikely. Vendor offerings may come and go, but now many established "user" companies have substantial initiatives in the cognitive space. And those who understand cognitive technologies and are aware of their business role are positive about them, to say the least.

From the 2017 Deloitte "cognitive aware" survey that I mentioned in the previous chapter, here are a few findings that suggest how bullish managers are about the potential of this technology in their businesses:

• 88 percent of respondents agreed that cognitive technologies are either "important" or "very important" to product and service offerings
• 93 percent felt that they are important or very important to internal business processes
• 76 percent believed that cognitive technologies will "substantially transform" their companies within the next three years
• 57 percent said their industries would transform during the same period
• None of the respondents believed that cognitive technologies won't drive substantive change, either for themselves or their industry

These don't sound like numbers for a technology likely to take a dive. We also found in the survey that the more experience respondents had with cognitive technology, the more positive they were about it.

I will describe several other surveys from vendors and consulting firms throughout this book, but none expresses more clearly the positive feelings of executives in large enterprises.

Of course, not every organization and manager has embraced the technology. Many don't know much about it yet. In order to find 250 senior managers in large organizations for the Deloitte survey, we had to contact 1,507 managers. Some were eliminated from the survey for reasons other than unfamiliarity with AI, but 56 percent were screened out because they were not knowledgeable about the technologies or their companies were not active with them.

Similarly, in a 2017 McKinsey survey with 3,073 respondents, only 20 percent said they had adopted one or more AI-related technology at scale or in a core part of their business.[1] Others were experimenting, of course, but were not yet seriously engaged with the technology. Almost every survey suggests that a high degree of enthusiasm about AI exists, but that it's still early days in terms of broad corporate application. Some far-sighted businesses, however, are playing the bellwether role.

The Broad Rationale for Cognitive Technology in Business

Why should business managers and professionals learn about cognitive technologies and put them to work? Some economists argue that recent technologies haven't had the impact of older ones like trains, automobiles, and electricity, which may well be true. But technologies that can think and act with a high degree of autonomy would seem to offer plenty of potential productivity gains. We haven't had much productivity growth in the United States, Europe, or other advanced economies over the past decade. Not since the mid-1970s has productivity growth in the United States reached 3 percent or so, and over the last decade it has grown at an annual rate of 1.2 percent. The last two years it has grown at only about half that dismal rate, and Europe's annual productivity growth is even less at about 0.5 percent of late.

Of course, increased productivity means that the same amount of work can be done by fewer workers. Many fear that with productivity increases from cognitive tools might also come substantial job losses.

On the other hand, cognitive technologies could counteract the negative impact of aging workforces and declining labor force participation as well. I'll address these issues in greater detail in chapter 8. But thus far it appears that the impact of cognitive technologies on the labor force will be marginal and slow. And we need productivity to grow our economies and increase the standard of living.

Cognitive technologies are specifically aimed at knowledge work processes within organizations, and these have been particularly important and problematic in terms of productivity. As Peter Drucker argued as far back as 1959 (when he coined the term *knowledge worker*), knowledge work productivity is the key to economic success in the twenty-first century. And Drucker also pointed out that the professions with the highest percentage of knowledge workers—healthcare, education, and professional services—have some of the worst productivity improvement rates. Witness, for example, the very high cost of healthcare and college education in our society. If some of these tasks could be performed by smart machines—and they can—wouldn't it be good for all or most of us?

Knowledge work productivity within organizations has been a long-term interest of mine—I wrote a book on it called *Thinking for a Living* in 2005—and until recently there were relatively few examples of smart machines that help with the topic. But many jobs and processes could be transformed with them.

The Cognitive Advantage in Healthcare
Take, for example, the process of medical diagnosis and treatment. As I pointed out in chapter 1, IBM has been working for several years to use Watson to diagnose cancer and recommend treatments for it. Watson hasn't fully succeeded yet, but IBM and the pathbreaking medical centers who are implementing Watson are making progress toward this very important objective. The primary focus of the effort is to learn from the vast amount of medical and scientific research published—about 2.5 million new research articles each year. Learning from those could mean higher cure rates, as well as greater access to the best care even in remote locations. That was one of the reasons why Memorial Sloan

Kettering Cancer Center decided to work with Watson—to make widely available the level of knowledge of the hospital's best oncologists to the world at large.

There could also be major progress in diagnosing disease with medical imaging. Computer-aided diagnosis (CAD) using MRI, CAT, or ultrasound devices is already as good as many human radiologists, according to multiple studies. But this has not yet led to lower costs for imaging, which accounts for about 10 percent of all healthcare costs in the United States.[2] Even better diagnostic accuracy, which seems likely with deep learning–based image recognition, might lead the imaging industry to rely more heavily on CAD. Big vendors like IBM, several startups, large imaging machine providers like GE, and various academic medical centers are all working assiduously on better image-based diagnosis. Considerable work will be needed on standards for the use of these technologies in clinical care before they make a real impact, but the opportunity is there.

Cognitive technologies could also make prescription drugs cheaper and bring them to market faster. It takes about twelve years for a pharmaceutical firm to research, develop, test, and launch a product. Several firms, including Pfizer, Novartis, and Celgene, are working with IBM Watson to try to identify and bring new drugs to market faster. The jury is still out on whether this will work.

Firms like Pfizer are also using machine learning to analyze patient and physician data to learn which types of approaches are most successful for patients. The company built a model that leveraged anonymized longitudinal prescribing data from physicians. After examining thousands of variables with machine learning, the analysis revealed that physicians who were optimally titrating (identifying the most effective dosage of) one of Pfizer's medicines had better patient outcomes. They shared these insights with the sales force to enable more patient-centric and customized conversations in the office, and built them into their digital messaging channels to ensure meaningful messages to support the patient population. The data are updated every six months to ensure relevancy and inform resourcing decisions.

Many Industries, Many Functions

Of course, key business activities in many other industries outside of healthcare could be transformed by cognitive technologies, and some already have been. Marketing and sales, for example, could be accomplished with much greater precision than is currently possible; salespeople can call on the customers where deals are most likely to close. Machine learning could analyze and constantly update "propensity to buy" models that predict which customers are most likely to buy certain products and services. Companies like Cisco Systems and IBM already create tens of thousands of models of this type with machine learning. Cisco, for example, went from generating tens of "artisanal" or human-created propensity models to about 60,000 autonomously generated ones. A small group of analysts and data scientists in a group called Global Customer Insights generates these models each quarter using machine learning. Every potential customer—more than a hundred million of them—of every Cisco product in every country is represented in those models, which is why so many different models are required. Cisco's sales and marketing teams use the models to decide which products to offer to which customers.[3] In fact, they relied so heavily on them that Cisco had to implement a more powerful IT capability to generate the models early enough in the quarter for salespeople to take advantage of them.

In digital marketing, machine learning is already used to target particular publishers and individual customers with digital ads. Thousands of models a week are created for this purpose. It's often difficult to interpret so many complex models, but the stakes are low enough (pennies per ad placement) so that the reason a particular ad is placed on a particular site doesn't matter very much.

Other firms are working on marketing applications of machine learning that increase customer engagement. Macy's, for example, is working with both IBM's Watson and Cognitive Scale, an Austin-based AI vendor, to improve personalization and engagement on its website and mobile app. The Cognitive Scale technology uses a game to build a personal profile of apparel that the customer likes. The Watson technology, called Macy's OnCall, answers customer questions on the mobile app in natural language and guides customers to desired sections within physical stores. Used on its Macys.com website, the conversational agent can deal with straightforward text-based queries like "Where is my order?" and "How do I return this product?" The agent already handles more than 25 percent of customer queries on the site, and can pass customers on to a human agent if necessary. Macy's is also exploring similar technologies in its call center.[4]

Working with a startup called ModeAI, Levi's is using machine learning and deep learning image recognition to power a "Virtual Stylist," the goal of which is to make online shopping as engaging as visiting a store. It combines a conversational interface with a visual focus to engage the customer in getting the right fit for jeans and other Levi's products. The system also scrapes the web and social media content to allow customers to see how other people are using Levis across the globe.

In customer service, natural language processing applications from firms like IBM (the Watson Virtual Agent) and IPsoft's Amelia are increasingly answering customer questions. They offer the possibility of better answers at any time of the day, with no waiting. One large U.S. bank, for example, gets two billion calls to its call centers every year, and it is looking to Amelia to answer at least the relatively easy questions—balance inquiries and transfers, for example—for many of those customers.

The same technologies are also being used within organizations to interface with employees. Got a question about your healthcare coverage or your vacation balance for your human resources organization? Need to reset your password or report a printer outage to your IT organization? Chances are good that IT and HR questions will soon be directed to a smart machine, rather than a person. Companies like ServiceNow, which already handle many such issues with automation technology, are adding machine learning to their offerings to make them more intelligent. Many human employees don't really enjoy answering the same questions over and over, so they may not mind losing this responsibility.

Companies are also employing cognitive technologies in the supply chain. Traditional optimization technologies that helped to predict inventory levels and avoid out-of-stocks, for example, are being replaced by machine learning systems that can continuously monitor sales, weather, and responses to marketing promotions to adjust supply chains. Companies like UPS are replacing fixed daily routes with dynamic ones adjusted in real time for weather and traffic—again with machine learning. Only cognitive technologies can handle all the necessary data. And at some point supply chains may be powered by autonomously driven trucks, which will bring enormous changes to that domain.

Finally, manufacturing companies are benefitting from cognitive technologies as well. Some, of course, are embedding cognitive technologies in their products. As I'll discuss in chapter 4, cognitively enhanced products are an objective of a surprisingly large number of firms. Vehicles, telecommunications and computing devices, industrial machinery, home appliances—all of these could be platforms for AI applications at some point, and many are already, if on a small scale. Automobile and truck manufacturers, of course, are rapidly trying to make their vehicles more autonomous. That dream would be impossible without cognitive technologies.

But cognitive technology is also being used to transform various aspects of the manufacturing process itself. Robots continually become more collaborative and flexible. They increasingly have the intelligence that only cognitive systems can provide. And as they start to communicate and learn from each other, their intelligence will mushroom (what an influential paper by Gill Pratt, head of the Toyota Research Institute, calls a "Cambrian explosion" of robotic intelligence).[5]

And cognitive technologies are also being used to make industrial machines more efficient and reliable. A number of companies are pursuing this goal, but GE is the most visible. All data from sensors in GE's jet engines, gas turbines, windmills, MRI and CAT scanners, and so on are captured and stored in a *digital twin* model. The model can then diagnose faults and predict the need for maintenance, ultimately reducing or eliminating unplanned downtime in that machine. The digital twin concept can be extended to aggregations of machines—a plant or fleet can be digitally twinned as well.

The data never stop flowing into the digital twin models, and there can be a lot of variables in them. We may also see change over time in what variables and models predict the need for maintenance. Machine learning is clearly the best technology in such situations. It can learn from new data and modify predictive models over time. This cognitive technology can also identify anomalies, signatures, and trends in machine performance, and understand a pattern of behavior or learn efficiencies within a machine and use that as a best practice for other machines. GE already has about 750,000 digital twins and is rapidly adding more.

Of course, cognitive technologies can be applied to businesses in other areas. New product development, finance, information technology, and many other functions are already using these technologies. If a decision is to be made and there are plenty of structured numeric data to analyze in making it, machine learning is appropriate. If text or speech is to be analyzed, you can employ natural language processing. Got some images to identify? Deep learning is probably your answer. As you can imagine, there are hundreds or thousands of scenarios in business for which some form of AI will be appropriate. Not all will be a perfect fit, but the match is worth considering.

Why Only Big Companies and Tech Startups?

Thus far, the most aggressive adopters of AI have been "digital native" online businesses (Google, Facebook, etc.), large enterprises, and tech startups, many of which have some aspect of cognitive technology as the key differentiation for their businesses. There has been relatively little adoption by small to medium-sized firms that are not in technology-intensive industries. There are several reasons for this—some good, some not so good.

First of all, the pattern of AI adoption is not that different from other technologies. Tech firms adopt technologies early for obvious reasons. Startups build their businesses around new technologies. Large enterprises are typically next in line; they have the technological sophistication to make informed investments in new technologies, and can hire the people to build and implement new solutions.

Big data and analytics followed a similar adoption pattern; tech firms and large enterprises adopted them early as well. This particular adoption, it turns out, is critical for the successful adoption of cognitive technologies. Most cognitive technologies have statistics at their core, and if your organization hasn't done anything with statistics and analytics, it's probably not going to do much with AI either.

Large firms—particularly those with many consumers as customers— tend to have a lot of data on those customers and on the transactions done with them. Through their ongoing operations they generate substantial amounts of data on other aspects of the business. That's a big advantage in the ability to make use of cognitive methods and tools, which need a lot of data to work well. Smaller firms, and those with businesses rather than consumers as customers, are less likely to have the requisite data, at least about customers. However, business-to-business firms can increasingly do cognitive technology applications with machine data or some other type.

Company size may offer financial advantages that may assist large businesses in adopting AI. Some of the software can be expensive. While cognitive software programs are not always expensive—some are free as open source programs—the skills to work with them are not cheap.[6] Large firms can afford to pay proprietary vendors, expensive consultants, and expensive data scientists as employees. Smaller firms often can't.

Perhaps the key factor that is lacking in small to medium firms from an AI standpoint is awareness and understanding of what is possible. Big firms have people whose job it is to look out for promising new technologies and inject them into the organization; small firms usually don't. Managers in small to mid-size firms are often preoccupied with making products (or services), selling them, and getting them out the door. Even if cognitive technologies could make those processes much better, faster, or cheaper, they may not be aware of the opportunity. The most likely solution is for managers in small to mid-size firms to force themselves to take the time to look outward and forward—to technologies that could make their firms much more successful.

Of course, big companies have some disadvantages as well when it comes to integrating AI into their businesses. They typically have a set of legacy IT systems and well-developed business processes that drive and inform their activities. Integrating AI-based decisions and actions into them isn't easy. If, for example, a company has developed a new set of sales propensity models to identify the most likely buyers of particular products and services, integrating the recommendations into customer relationship management systems and processes, and into the behavior of salespeople, is not likely to be easy. Big companies often also have bureaucratic planning processes, and well-established capital allocation processes that don't change as often as they should. However, on the whole they are more likely to implement AI than small- to mid-size companies. And unfortunately for those smaller firms, AI is likely to help big companies get bigger.

More Than Testing the Waters, but Not a Deep Dive Yet

So just how committed are large firms to these technologies? On the whole, they're doing more than dipping a toe into the water, but not quite diving in. Many companies that are exploring cognitive technologies are doing so on a somewhat experimental basis. Jim Fowler, the chief information officer of GE, spoke for many large enterprises in saying (at the end of 2017) that in 2018, "We need to get intelligent about AI and move from experiment to solving real problems at scale."[7]

This experimental approach has several indications. The somewhat conservative spending levels on the technologies are one. Only 12 percent of the firms represented in the survey are investing $10 million or more on cognitive technologies. Roughly equal percentages—about 25 percent each—have spent $5 million to $10 million, $1 million to $5 million, or $500,000 to $1 million. Seven percent have spent less than $500,000. In another late 2017 survey by NewVantage Partners of fifty-nine very large organizations, 53 percent of responding firms were spending less than $50 million on both big data and AI initiatives. Enterprise uses of cognitive technologies are still in the early stages, and most organizations do not have well-defined budgets for them yet.

A survey of chief information officers in global organizations suggests an even more tentative approach to AI. Gartner performs an annual CIO survey, and not surprisingly, AI was a major focus in the 2018 survey (done in mid-2017). In that survey of over 3,100 CIOs, only 4 percent said they had already invested and deployed AI, but an additional 21 percent said they were "in short-term planning or actively experimenting." Another 25 percent had AI in their middle- or long-term plans. Forty-nine percent said AI was either of no interest or "on the radar, but no action planned."[8]

Companies represented in the Deloitte survey have both pilots/ proofs of concept and production implementations or deployments underway. Thirty-four percent of respondents had three to five pilots underway. In addition, 28 percent indicated "one or two" pilots, while 20 percent said "six to ten." In production applications, the numbers are somewhat smaller. "one or two" and "three to five" each received 31 percent. Companies with more projects reported greater levels of benefit (see figure 2.1). In an interview after the survey, one consumer

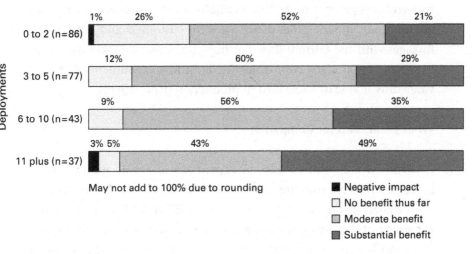

Figure 2.1
Numbers of AI Projects by Benefits Achieved
Source: 2017 Deloitte "Cognitive Aware" Survey

products firm mentioned that it was running several smaller pilots using machine learning, but they related to larger goals of understanding consumers in greater detail and determining the effectiveness of trade promotion and marketing spending.

Another indication of the commitment level of companies to AI is where they choose to implement it. High levels of commitment would involve using it to work directly with customers, or in revenue-generating functions like sales. Corporate function use—in IT, for example, which appeared first in the Deloitte survey, might indicate a lower level of commitment thus far. It's undoubtedly true that many firms are using technologies like autonomics to monitor and reboot servers, or intelligent agents to answer IT questions. This is important activity, but it's not likely to quicken the pulse of CEOs.

Some firms, of course, are using the technologies in customer-facing and operations-intensive applications. Product development/R&D was second to IT in the survey, with 44 percent checking that function. Customer service (40 percent), supply chain/procurement (38 percent), service operations (37 percent), and manufacturing (32 percent) were other functions commonly mentioned.

As companies grow more comfortable and experienced with cognitive technologies—and as the technologies themselves mature—we will undoubtedly see more direct use with customers and more direct linkages with the bottom line. For now, it's reasonable to experiment in the ways that many companies are. But those experiments will be of value only if at least some lead to production deployments.

What's Still Hard for Companies

A friend with several decades of experience in the IT industry once pointed out to me that the most valuable thing that authors could tell their readers about AI is that, "This s*** is still hard." Perhaps the hardest aspect of it is integrating cognitive technologies with existing systems and business processes. That was the conclusion of the survey of "cognitive aware" executives; in that survey, 47 percent of respondents said that they found it "difficult to integrate cognitive projects with existing processes and systems." Yet such integration is usually necessary if organizations are going to successfully deploy cognitive technologies into production applications.

For most AI applications, after a model is developed it needs to be deployed—embedded in, or called by, an existing system. It is often much easier to develop a model than to deploy it. Some vendors, such as the Canadian startup Element AI, say they are developing "AI as a service" offerings to ease the integration problem. As I'll discuss in chapter 7, another way to ease integration is to adopt the cognitive tools that vendors of major transaction systems—including enterprise resource planning, customer relationship management, and HR systems—are embedding in their applications.

In other challenges from the survey, 40 percent felt that "technologies and expertise are too expensive," and 37 percent complained that "managers don't understand cognitive technologies and how they work." In addition, 35 percent are challenged because they "can't get enough people with expertise in the technology." Smaller percentages feel that "technologies are immature" (31 percent) or that "technologies have been oversold in the marketplace" (18 percent).

Building some standalone applications with cognitive systems can be relatively straightforward, depending on the specific technology chosen. Not all of them are terribly hard; robotic process automation (RPA) is pretty easy to implement, for example, although large-scale adoption of RPA can be difficult to integrate with existing technologies and change the resulting architectures over time. Statistical machine learning using labeled training data isn't that tough to do for anyone with some analytical training. Rule-based systems are relatively easy to develop for small-scale applications.

But other aspects of working with cognitive technology are still pretty difficult for most organizations. Deep learning, for example, is only moderately difficult to program on a computer, but it requires a lot of labeled data to come up with an effective model—and as I have noted, the result is largely uninterpretable—even for PhD data scientists. In general, to use the technology effectively usually requires a high degree of expertise—which is difficult and expensive to source.

For computers to make sense of language is still a generally difficult area. From IBM Watson ads one gets the impression that all you have to do is feed text or speech into Watson, and out comes insights or smart answers to questions. This is not generally the case. There usually needs to be considerable activity to structure the language before a machine can do much with it. As my friend Seth Earley, the CEO of Earley Information Sciences, put it in an article, "there is no AI without IA" (information architecture).[9]

For example, Morgan Stanley has developed a new system—similar in concept to the one I described at DBS, and based on machine learning—to identify investment opportunities that its financial advisors can present to clients. The system works well, but Morgan Stanley would like to add the capability to mine the reports that its investment analysts produce in order to make recommendations to clients. However, each analyst writes in a different style, and there is relatively little common structure to the reports. According to the bank's technology experts, there is no technology that can extract the salient comments from these reports and use them in a cognitive application. The only recourse they know of is to persuade investment analysts to structure their documents more effectively and all write with a common format—and they think that would be a request that the analysts would find highly unappealing. At the moment, offshore outsourcers are "curating" the documents to put them into a common format.

This difficulty of structuring human language is one of the reasons that IBM Watson projects have often taken much longer, and cost much more, than organizations expect. Particularly if you are the first to adopt the technology in your industry, you will have to teach Watson the language of your industry and find a way to structure the knowledge you want it to absorb. This may also be true for other types of natural language processing applications.

Intelligent agents are somewhat easier to employ, but they can be difficult to get to work at a high enough level to turn customers over to them. That typically requires a company to develop a taxonomy of terms that might come up in an interaction with an agent and the relationships between them—a *dialog graph*. If you're the first in your industry to do this, it's going to take a few months at least. Even if someone else in your industry has done it and a vendor makes it available to you, there will still probably be a need for customization.

Overall, it's important for anyone implementing cognitive technologies to be aware that they are still somewhat immature. Progress is being made quickly in the current environment, but if your application is on the frontier of that progress you may encounter substantial technical challenges. Before you start with a particular project you may want to assess just how close to the frontier you are likely to come.

Despite these and other challenges, some firms are adopting cognitive applications and moving ahead smartly with them. The next chapter is about what they are doing and how they are making progress, even with technologies that will still benefit from further development.

3   What Are Companies Doing Today?

In this chapter, I'll describe what is actually happening today among large enterprises and their use of AI.[1] I'll discuss which current approaches to AI are being implemented (and in what numbers), what underlying technologies are being employed, the business objectives of these projects, and the levels of success achieved thus far. Then, since it's still early days for enterprise AI, I'll suggest what key activities companies are pursuing to build up their cognitive capabilities.

This analysis is based largely on a study of 152 consulting projects employing cognitive technologies that I undertook with a team from Deloitte. Most of the projects had been undertaken by Deloitte consulting and advisory services teams, and were primarily (although not exclusively) in North America. A few were projects I was involved in personally, several of which were in Europe. The analysis was done in mid-2017; the projects took place in 2016 and 2017.

An Overview of the Cognitive Project Landscape

Figure 3.1 has a collection of data about where AI activity is taking place from the 152 cognitive projects. Of course, the projects don't come from a random sample, and may partially result from differential emphases on cognitive technologies within particular industry groups at Deloitte, or the structure of the firm's business. As might be expected, most projects are from data-intensive industries like financial services and life sciences/healthcare. Relatively few are from media and telecom companies—which also have substantial amounts of data—and energy/utility firms. Just

PROJECTS BY INDUSTRY

Consumer and Industrial Products	24	Energy and Resources	5
Financial Services	47	Federal	12
Life Sciences/ Healthcare	37	Public Sector	3
Technology, Media, and Telecom	13	Other	11
		TOTAL	**152**

Clients were primarily concentrated in 3 sectors—Financial Services (31%), Life Sciences and Healthcare (25%), and Consumer and Industrial Products (16%)—which accounted for nearly three-quarters of all engagements studied.

MOST COMMON EXECUTIVE SPONSOR

LEVEL		
20	**18**	**11**
C-Suite	VP	Director
		TOTAL 49

Sponsors for these cognitive engagements were often found at the executive level, illustrating that cognitive is truly a priority for today's business leaders.

MOST COMMON FUNCTIONAL AREA

Multiple	24	Risk	9
Operations	19	Tax	8
Customer	13	Supply chain	7
Sector-specific	11	Workforce	1
Finance	11	Technology	1
		TOTAL	**104**

Cognitive projects were typically spanned across multiple functional areas, highlighting the need for enterprise-wide alignment and buy-in.

Figure 3.1
Industries, Sponsors, and Functions for Cognitive Projects
Source: Analysis of 152 AI consulting projects

under 10 percent are in the public sector, with most coming from the U.S. federal government. Most of these government projects involve robotic process automation.

In terms of the business functions at which cognitive projects are targeted, the most common category was a combination of functions—connecting finance and supply chain, for example, by comparing invoices from suppliers to items actually shipped. Operations and customer-oriented projects (marketing and sales) were the two most common individual functions.

The most common project sponsors for which a sponsor was recorded are "C-suite" senior executives. VPs and directors are also commonly sponsoring projects. Perhaps the most interesting aspect of this exhibit is the breadth of functions to which AI is being applied. In addition to those listed, I have heard about projects in corporate legal, corporate security, and strategy.

Three Types of AI Capabilities

Since the technologies for AI can be somewhat confusing and over-lapping, it can be useful to look at AI through the lens of *business capabilities* rather than *technologies*. Broadly speaking, AI can support three important business activities:

• Automating structured and repetitive work processes, often via robotics or robotic process automation.
• Gaining insight through extensive analysis of structured data, most often using machine learning.
• Engaging with customers and employees, using natural language processing chatbots, intelligent agents, and machine learning.

Process Automation

The automation of digital and physical tasks—most often back-office administrative and financial activities—was the most common activity we found (71 of 152 projects, or forty-seven percent). Physical robots fall into this category, but most of the projects analyzed involved robotic process automation performing structured back-office digital tasks. These capabilities are advances on earlier business-process automation because the "robots" (actually code on a server) act like a human inputting and consuming information from multiple IT systems. Examples include:

• Transferring data from email and call center systems into systems of record—for example, requests for address changes or new service additions
• Replacing lost credit or ATM cards without human intervention, reaching into multiple systems to update records and handle customer communications
• Reconciling failures to charge for services across different bank billing systems by extracting information from multiple document types
• "Reading" legal and contractual documents to extract contract provisions using natural language processing
• Producing automated investment content (a few paragraphs about how customer investments have performed over the last period) for wealth management customers at insurance companies

These projects are common in part because RPA is the least expensive and easiest to implement of automation technologies, and typically brings a quick and high return on investment. These applications aren't programmed to learn and improve, but vendors are slowly adding more intelligence and learning capability to them. Some experts refer to the overall technology category as *robotic and cognitive automation*, but I'm not sure the "cognitive" component is deserved yet. RPA is particularly well suited to working across multiple back-end systems, and doesn't require re-architecting of those systems.

Some users are developing multiple process-automation robots for different purposes. At NASA, for example, cost pressures led the agency to launch four RPA pilots in accounts payable and receivable, IT spending, and human resources—all managed by a shared services center. All four projects worked well and are being rolled out across the organization. In the human resource application, for example, 86 percent of transactions were completed without human intervention. NASA is now implementing more RPA bots, some with higher levels of intelligence. As Jim Walker, project leader for the shared services organization notes, "So far it's not rocket science" (and someone at NASA should know).

One might imagine that robotic process automation would quickly replace administrative employees. But across the seventy-one projects we reviewed (including at NASA), that wasn't a primary objective or common outcome. Only a few projects led to staff reductions, and these were primarily of outsourced workers. In only one case did we hear of plans to use RPA to eliminate substantial numbers of internal jobs. That said, I do expect cognitive and robotic automation projects to lead to some job loss in the future. The offshore business process outsourcing industry is likely to be the hardest hit. If you can outsource a process to people thousands of miles away, you can probably automate it with RPA.

The technology of RPA is relatively easy to use, but the challenges of implementing it come primarily from the business process. Companies should have a good understanding of both their existing business processes and the new processes they want RPA to enable before implementing the technology. But most companies don't do that. David Brain, a cofounder of the RPA consulting firm Symphony Ventures, argues that companies need to do process design and engineering work on virtually every RPA project—what we have referred to as "putting the process back in RPA."

Brain argues that process work is essential to an effective RPA implementation for several reasons, including these:

• The existing process is often overly complex, with unnecessary steps that could be eliminated before RPA is implemented.

• RPA involves the codification of business rules, but existing business rules often haven't been examined for many years and don't make sense in the current environment.

• There are often existing business rules that are described by those who perform them as "judgment," but in actuality they can be turned into more accurate and consistent algorithms.

• The level of process knowledge and understanding within companies is generally low. The companies may have collections of standard operating procedures (SOPs), but they are often poorly documented and out of date.

• RPA often supports "swivel chair" processes that involve a lot of back-and-forth access to information systems, but in many cases the process could extract all the necessary information at once from a system—i.e., with less swiveling.

• There are often built-in checkpoints for human processes that are no longer needed with RPA—because at least after the initial kinks are ironed out of the system, computer systems don't generally make mistakes.

• Many companies have cut out steps from existing processes that add customer value, but are dropped because they don't have the necessary resources. For example, in-process communications with customers about the state of their orders or applications may be time-consuming for human workers to send and receive, but are very easy for process robots.

With changes like these, a process enabled by RPA can become much more efficient and effective than the previous one. And while it is likely that some human functions will be taken over by RPA, in most companies implementing the technology thus far there has been relatively little impact on staffing. Whether they remain so will be an important factor to monitor in understanding the impact of this form of AI.

Cognitive Insight

Applications that use algorithms to detect patterns in vast volumes of structured data and interpret its meaning—think of it as "analytics on steroids"—are the second broad AI category in business (57 of 152 projects, or 37 percent). This is the oldest category of artificial intelligence, since machine learning—the typical underlying technology for cognitive insight—has been available for several decades. It is both more common and more automated than in the past, however. It's necessary when there is a large amount of data and many possible predictors of a phenomenon to be predicted or classified. Some examples of how cognitive insight is being employed include:

• Predicting what a particular customer is likely to buy (customer propensity modeling)
• Identifying credit fraud in real time, and insurance claims fraud
• Analyzing warranty data to identify safety or quality problems in automobiles and other manufactured products
• Gathering and analyzing sensor data to predict when an industrial machine will malfunction
• Automating personalized targeting of digital ads
• Providing insurers with more accurate and detailed actuarial modeling

Cognitive insights provided by machine learning differ from those available from traditional analytics in three ways: They are usually much more data-intensive and detailed, the models need to be trained in most cases on some part of the available data, and they can learn—improving their ability to use new data to make predictions or put things into categories. As I mentioned in the last chapter, versions of machine learning (deep learning in particular) can also perform feats such as recognizing images and speech.

Cognitive insight applications are typically used to improve performance on jobs only machines can do—tasks such as programmatic ad buying involving such high-speed data crunching and automation that they've long been beyond human ability. Therefore, they are unlikely to put humans out of their jobs.

A less obvious application of cognitive insight involves the use of machine learning to integrate data for better analytics. While the activity of curating data has historically been quite labor-intensive, now machine learning can identify probabilistic matches—data likely to be about the same person or company, but in slightly different formats—across databases. GE has used this technology (from Tamr, a company I advise) to integrate supplier data and has saved $80 million in its first year by eliminating redundancies and negotiating contracts that were previously managed at the business unit level. GE is now applying the same approach to customer and product data. Similarly, a large bank used this technology to extract data on terms from supplier contracts and match it with invoice numbers, identifying tens of millions of dollars in mismatches. A professional services audit practice is using cognitive insight to extract terms from audit-related contracts, which enables an audit to address a much higher proportion of documents, often 100 percent, without human auditors having to painstakingly read through them.

The primary constraints to this form of cognitive activity are the availability of large volumes of data, some of which must be "labeled" in terms of knowing the outcome to be predicted. For example, if an organization is trying to use sensor data to predict when a machine will break down (for purposes of predictive maintenance), it has to have a substantial number of actual breakdowns from which it can learn. This form of learning from labeled data, called *supervised learning*, comprises the great majority of business uses of cognitive insights.

Cognitive Engagement

These applications, the least common of the three (24 of 152 projects, or sixteen percent), engage employees and customers by providing them with rich language or image-based personalized information and services. This category includes:

• Intelligent agents that offer 24/7 customer service addressing a broad and growing array of service issues from password requests to technical support questions—all in the customer's natural language

- Internal service sites for answering employee questions on topics including IT issues, employee benefits, and HR policy questions
- Product and service recommendation systems for retailer websites that increase personalization, engagement, and sales—typically with rich language or images
- Health treatment recommendation systems (often offered by insurance companies) that help providers create customized care plans that take individual patients' health status and previous treatments into account

Engagement-oriented applications for use by employees are currently more common than those for use by customers. That may change as firms become more comfortable turning customer interactions over to machines. Vanguard, for example, piloted an intelligent agent that helped its customer service staff answer frequently asked questions posed by customers. Over time, the plan is to allow customers to engage with a cognitive agent directly, rather than with the human service agents. In the early days of the pilot, however, the project was taking too much time for human agents to access and use. Becton, Dickinson (BD) in the United States is using the life-like intelligent agent avatar Amelia to serve as an internal employee help desk for IT support. It also plans to extend the use of the agent to customers at some point.

Skandinaviska Enskilda Banken (SEB) in the Nordic countries started its use of intelligent agents with an internal IT help desk application, but then made Aida, a Swedish-speaking avatar based on Amelia, available to banking customers on a limited basis in order to test her performance and customer response. The move is part of a broader objective to shift to digital channels for customer support. The bank's goal is not to replace human employees but to provide 24/7 service and facilitate growth without adding employees.[2]

The conservative approach that these companies are taking to customer-facing cognitive service is due in part to the technology's immaturity. Facebook, for example, found in 2017 that its Messenger chatbots couldn't answer 70 percent of customer requests without human intervention.[3] As a result, Facebook and several other firms are restricting bot-based interfaces to certain topic domains or conversation types.

Customers are not particularly pleased about the current state of chatbot capabilities either. According to a Chatbots.org survey of U.S. and U.K. consumers conducted in late 2017, over half of respondents in both countries were bothered by having to repeat information given to a chatbot when escalated to a human agent.[4] About a third felt that chatbots had a problem with "getting stuck and not knowing what to do next." As a result, over half of the respondents found chatbots to be "not effective" or only "somewhat effective." Clearly there is a need for cognitive engagement applications to up their game.

Perhaps in part because of technological immaturity, I have not heard of a single customer service or sales representative who has lost a job to a cognitive-engagement app, nor are the organizations I have researched planning major layoffs in the near future. Their typical goal is to use this technology to handle growing numbers of employee and customer interactions without adding staff. Some organizations are planning to transition customer-support personnel to more complex activities that bots can't yet do including handling customer issues that escalate, conducting extended unstructured dialogues, or reaching out to customers before they call in with problems. Many agents say they would be happy to hand over routine communications to machines.

Combining Categories

Even within categories, cognitive tools are increasingly being broken down into components and application program interfaces (APIs) to perform specific tasks. IBM's Watson, which many think of as a monolithic question-answering machine, is really a collection of APIs. APIs are available either as off-the-shelf applications that do specific jobs (typically from proprietary vendors like IBM) or as open-source applications that users can modify. This flexibility allows organizations to integrate and assemble components to achieve objectives, which often cross and combine the categories above. But doing so requires substantial effort and expertise.

One such combined tool set was developed for an Italian insurer that wanted a "cognitive help desk" within its IT organization. This is a cognitive engagement application, but since many problems are still too difficult to be fully addressed by cognitive technology, the solution needed to be augmented by human help-desk representatives. Thus the company also needed robotic process automation to route problems to the right source of human expertise within IT. Finally, the system had to support Italian language text, which was not possible using many natural-language processing (NLP) tools.

This cognitive help desk uses unsupervised deep learning technology, part of the "cognitive insights" category, from the vendor LoopAI Labs (where I am an advisor) as its primary cognitive tool. The software— which as an unsupervised learning tool is relatively unusual—can examine a collection of text documents in any language and identify key concepts, frequently asked questions and answers, previously resolved cases that are relevant to a problem at hand, and sections within key documents where a needed solution is most likely to be found. When combined with the "smart routing" capabilities of robotic process automation, the system has dramatically cut the resolution time (by 35 percent to 70 percent, depending on the type of question) and improved the accuracy of responses (now 70 percent to 85 percent, depending on the question) to help desk tickets.

Steps to Becoming a Cognitive Corporation

A key aspect of "what's happening now" with AI in business is not only applications, but capabilities. Many large enterprises are clearly beginning to build ongoing capabilities with cognitive technologies and becoming "cognitive corporations." Some of the capabilities to which they aspire are driven by the strategic and performance opportunities that cognitive technologies offer, but some are driven by the challenges that organizations have faced as they implemented their first cognitive projects.

It is early days for this transition, but it's already clear that it is happening and what some of the key capabilities are. They include:

• Understanding which technologies perform what types of tasks
• Building on current strengths in big data and analytics

- Creating a prioritized portfolio of technology matched to processes and tasks
- Creating a series of pilot or proof-of-concept projects
- Engaging in cognitive work redesign using design-thinking principles
- Focusing on scaling and achieving productivity benefits

Understanding Technologies and Tasks

It's important to understand which technologies perform what types of tasks, and the strengths and limitations of each. I've described the different technologies and their functions in chapter 1, but organizations and managers need to internalize them. "Managers don't understand cognitive technologies and how they work" was cited as a challenge to their successful implementation by 37 percent of respondents in one survey, and I encounter this issue in many of the companies I work with.

It's easy to make mistakes if you don't understand the tradeoffs behind each technology. Rule-based expert systems and robotic process automation, for example, are transparent in how they do their work, but neither is capable of learning and improving. Deep learning, on the other hand, is great at learning from large volumes of labeled data, but it's almost impossible to understand how it creates the models it does. This "black box" issue can be problematic in highly regulated industries like financial services, in which regulators insist on knowing why a decision is made in a certain way.

As I noted in chapter 1, natural language processing has two alternative underlying technologies: one is a "brute force" statistical approach that requires a lot of data (Google Translate is one of the best examples), and the other is a more "semantic" approach requiring description of a "knowledge graph" of terms and relationships in the relevant topic domain. The creation of a knowledge graph tends to be a time-consuming and labor-intensive effort, particularly if the company or the vendor is doing it for the first time in a particular knowledge domain. Statistical approaches to NLP will work well for a company with a lot of data (say, from call center conversations that have been translated into text); the approach requires little data, but a lot of up-front architecting by human experts.

Understanding these technologies and tradeoffs will inform decisions about which might best address specific needs, which vendors to work with, and how quickly a system of a given type can be implemented. I have encountered several organizations that have wasted time and money pursuing the wrong technology for the job at hand. Acquiring this understanding requires ongoing research and education, usually from an IT or innovation group. Some of the heads of AI groups I have come across say they spend the majority of their time evangelizing for and explaining the differences among different types of cognitive technologies. That suggests that such individuals need to be as good at communicating as they are at data science and programming. I recommend that a company become familiar with at least the tool categories described in chapter 1.

Building on Current Analytical Strengths
Many cognitive technologies have statistical analysis and big data analytics at their core, so it's important for an organization to leverage those capabilities if it already has them. Few professionals have AI backgrounds and expertise at this point, so data scientists with statistical and big-data skills are most likely to be able to learn the nuts and bolts of these technologies and help develop and apply them to meet organizational goals. This is particularly true if the technologies being employed are some variation on statistical machine learning, which is a relatively easy extension of predictive analytics in many cases. A main factor in the success of these data science types is their willingness to learn new skills and methods. Some will leap at the opportunity, while others will want to stick with techniques learned in graduate school. Strive to have a high percentage of the former.

If you have traditional data science or analytics groups, consider putting them at the center of your AI efforts, which will likely tap expertise throughout the organization. Whether these efforts are narrow, short-term projects or broader, ongoing initiatives, the capabilities within these groups will prove essential to progress. If you don't have such groups in-house, you'll probably have to build an ecosystem of external AI-services providers that can supply the needed capability in the near term. Longer term, if you expect to be doing ongoing work with AI, you will want to recruit an expert in-house staff.

Given the scarcity of cognitive technology talent, most organizations should establish a centralized pool of resources—perhaps in a central service function like IT or strategy—and make experts available to high-priority projects. Later on, as needs and talent proliferate, it may make sense to have groups dedicated to particular business functions or units, but even then a central coordinating function can be useful in managing projects and careers. Many organizations already have central (or centrally coordinated) analytics teams, so it should be relatively easy to add AI skills to them.

Creating a Prioritized Portfolio of Projects

It's critical to engage in systematic evaluation of needs and capabilities before launching an AI program. In the companies I have studied, this was usually done in a workshop or other small consulting engagement that examined three broad areas. Several vendors and consulting firms offer such workshops.

The domain assessment looks at the business domains that could benefit most from cognitive applications. Typically those are parts of the company where some type of knowledge—insight derived from data analysis or a "corpus" of text—would be highly useful, but is not as available as needed.

• *Knowledge bottlenecks*—In some cases, the unavailability of knowledge is due to a bottleneck; knowledge exists somewhere, but is not optimally distributed. That's often the case in healthcare, for example, where knowledge is often siloed within practices or departments, or restricted to urban academic medical centers. Memorial Sloan Kettering Cancer Center expects, for example, that the primary benefits of its Watson-based cancer treatment program will come not from usage within the New York–based hospital itself (where there are many expert oncologists), but rather in remote clinics and distant regions where expertise is scarce.

• *Scaling challenges*—In other cases, knowledge is developable but the process is too slow or expensive to scale. Such is the case with knowledge developed by expensive brokers or financial advisors. In response, many investment and wealth management firms have developed AI-supported "robo-advice" capabilities that cost-effectively provide clients with routine sorts of financial guidance.

In the pharmaceutical industry, Pfizer is using IBM's Watson to accelerate drug-discovery research in immuno-oncology, an emerging approach to cancer treatment that uses the body's immune system to help fight cancer. Immuno-oncology drugs can be highly effective, but they can take up to twelve years to bring to market in part because the discovery process is so laborious. The company has tapped into Watson's machine learning, natural language processing, and other cognitive reasoning technologies to support the identification of new drug targets, combination therapies for study, and patient selection strategies. By combining Watson's capabilities for fast literature review with Pfizer's own data such as lab reports, AI is helping researchers look across disparate data sets to surface relationships and reveal hidden patterns that may speed the identification and development of this new class of drugs.

• *Inadequate firepower*—Finally, knowledge or insights might be in short supply because the amount of data is too much for human or existing computer firepower to adequately analyze and apply. This is the case when a firm has big data on consumers' digital behavior but a shortage of insight about what it means or how it can be strategically applied. To address this, companies are using machine learning to support programmatic buying of personalized digital ads, or, in the case of some business-to-business firms like Cisco Systems and IBM, to create tens of thousands of "propensity models" for determining which customers are likely to buy which products.

The *use case assessment* evaluates the use cases in which cognitive applications would generate substantial value and contribute to business success. Each case is an application of AI to a business problem. Prioritization of use cases should be based on factors such as how critical to strategy it is to address the targeted problem, how much change the application would bring about, and how difficult it would be to implement the proposed AI solution—both technically and organizationally. After use cases are constructed, they can be compared according to which offer the most short- and long-term value, and which might ultimately be built into a broader platform or suite of cognitive capabilities providing competitive advantage. Since cognitive tools typically support individual tasks, they have to be strung together to support an entire business process or even an entire job.

The *technology assessment* examines whether the AI being considered for each use case is truly up to the task. Chatbots and intelligent agents, for example, may frustrate some companies because most of them can't yet match human problem solving beyond simple scripted cases (although they are improving rapidly). Other technologies like robotic process automation that can streamline manual production systems such as invoicing may in fact slow down more complex processes. And deep learning visual recognition systems, while they can recognize images in photos and videos, require lots of labeled data and may be unable to make sense of a complex visual field. This gap between current and desired AI capabilities is not always immediately obvious. Thus most companies today are piloting cognitive applications, or using them in restricted situations, rather than rolling them out across the entire enterprise.

In time, cognitive technologies will transform how companies do business. Today, however, it's wiser to take incremental steps with the currently available technology while planning for transformational change in the not-too-distant future. You may ultimately want to turn routine customer interactions over to bots, for example, but for the time being it's likely more feasible—and sensible—to automate your internal IT help desk as a step toward the ultimate goal.

Creating Pilots or Proofs-of-Concept

Companies worldwide are undertaking proof-of-concept projects or pilots to explore the impacts of cognitive technologies. This is a good idea if the projects have high potential business value and if they allow the organization to test multiple different technologies. Some such projects can be pieces of potentially larger and more ambitious plans; some can stand alone. Pfizer, for example, has over a hundred projects across the company that employ some form of cognitive technology; many are pilots, and some are now in production.

Pilot projects should be selected and prioritized using criteria described above. Take special care to avoid "injections" of projects by senior executives who have been influenced by technology vendors. Just because executives and boards of directors may feel pressure to "do something cognitive" doesn't mean you should do something dumb. Because injected pilots don't go through a rigorous assessment process, they often fail, which can significantly set back the organization's AI program.

If the company plans to launch several pilots, consider creating a "cognitive center of excellence" or similar structure to manage them. This approach helps build the needed technology skills and capabilities within the organization, while also helping to move small pilots into broader production applications that will have a greater impact. At the medical technology giant BD, for example, a "Global Automation" function within the company's IT organization oversees a number of cognitive technology pilots, particularly employing intelligent digital agents and robotic process automation (the RPA work is done in partnership with the company's Global Shared Services organization). The group has developed a series of end-to-end process maps that guide cognitive-project implementation and help reveal automation opportunities. In addition, the function has developed graphical "heat maps" that indicate the organizational activities that are most amenable to AI interventions. BD has already successfully implemented intelligent agents in IT support processes, but does not believe that the technology can yet scale to support a large-scale enterprise processes like order-to-cash.

The health insurer Anthem has developed a similar function that it calls the Cognitive Capability Office. The company's chief information officer, Tom Miller (to whom the office reports), says that in establishing a centralized office for project prioritization, management, and review, Anthem is treating cognitive technology just like any other high-value business opportunity. The company is working on a variety of projects including robotic process automation systems, but the primary focus is to embed cognitive capabilities into a large-scale modernization of transaction systems. The company is standardizing, then automating, manual work in areas like claims.

Some firms embed their work on AI into a broader center for innovation and other new technologies. These are often separate from a company's headquarters and may be based in technology-oriented regions like Silicon Valley. Lowe's, for example, the home improvement retailer, established Lowe's Innovation Labs in the Seattle area. It pursues AI technologies primarily in the form of the LoweBot, a robot that can navigate the aisles of Lowe's stores autonomously. When customers are present in the stores, it can guide them to particular items they are seeking using voice recognition or a touchscreen display. When the stores are closed, the LoweBot doesn't retire for the evening, but rather spots misplaced items or low levels of inventory for items. LoweBots are being piloted in stores in Silicon Valley, where customers are presumably comfortable with technology.[5]

Sompo Holdings, an insurance company I mentioned in chapter 1, is also taking this broader innovation approach. It has a series of Sompo Digital Labs in Tokyo, Silicon Valley, and Tel Aviv. The Tokyo lab is exploring automated machine learning technology and IBM Watson; the Silicon Valley lab focuses on autonomous vehicles and other technologies, and the Tel Aviv lab focuses primarily on cybersecurity, including AI approaches to cybersecurity. The goal for each lab to work with AI and other technologies that can help to transform insurance and be incorporated into production deployments.

Engaging in Cognitive Work Redesign

As cognitive technologies are developed, organizations should think through how work will be done with a given new application, focusing specifically on the division of labor between humans and the AI. Some cognitive projects will involve 80 percent machine-based decisions and 20 percent human ones; others the converse. Systematic design activity is necessary to determine how humans and machines will augment each other's strengths and compensate for their weaknesses.

At the investment firm Vanguard, for example, a new Personal Advisor Services (PAS) offering combines automated investment advice and guidance from human advisors at a lower cost than purely human-advised investing. The PAS technology performs many of the traditional tasks of investment advising, including constructing a customized portfolio, rebalancing portfolios over time, tax loss harvesting, tax-efficient investment selection, and creating recommendations for safe withdrawal amounts for retirees. The system took over some tasks from advisors, including acquiring basic information from customers and presenting financial status information to them—tasks that were sometimes considered tedious for human advisors anyway.

Vanguard's advisory services requires customers to input more information about themselves than they traditionally had, and to furnish information about non-Vanguard assets to their advisor or directly to the system. It makes somewhat complex information (for example, about Monte Carlo simulations of how long a portfolio would last in retirement) directly available to customers, and allows customers to override actions that the automated system planned. Machine learning technology helps provide each customer with the likelihood that their retirement assets will outlive them.

For Vanguard's human advisors, several of whom helped develop PAS, the new work process required undertaking some new roles. The primary description of their new role was to be an "investing coach," able to answer investor questions, encourage healthy financial behaviors, and be, in Vanguard's words, "an emotional circuit breaker" to keep investors on their plan. Advisors are encouraged to learn about behavioral finance to perform these roles effectively. To keep costs down and preserve face-to-face contact with investors, advisors often employ videoconferencing technology for occasional meetings. The PAS approach has been highly successful, quickly gathering more than $100 billion in assets under management, and customer satisfaction with the offering is high. Contrary to the stereotype of who will gravitate toward automated advice, the majority of customers are over fifty-five.

While Vanguard understood the importance of work redesign when implementing cognitive technologies, many companies have simply "paved the cow path" by automating existing work processes, particularly when using robotic process automation technology (as I noted above in the section discussing that technology). Automating established workflows can be a fast way to get to implementation and ROI, but it does miss the opportunity to take full advantage of AI capabilities and substantially improve the process.

Cognitive work redesign benefits from applying design-thinking principles such as understanding customer or end-user needs, involving employees whose work will be restructured, treating designs as experimental "first drafts," considering multiple alternatives, and explicitly considering cognitive technology capabilities in the design process. Most cognitive projects will also benefit from more iterative, agile approaches to development, including of their work design components.

Focusing on Scaling and Achieving Productivity Benefits

Many organizations have successfully launched cognitive pilots, but for several reasons they haven't had as much success rolling them out at production scale. Most companies are just getting familiar with the technology, and it is not fully mature yet in many cases. And production usage of cognitive systems requires substantial modification of existing ways of working.

Detailed plans for scaling up, which requires collaboration between technology experts and owners of the business process being automated, need to be developed before rollout begins. Given that cognitive technologies typically support individual tasks rather than entire processes, scale-up almost always requires integration with existing systems and processes. Firms should examine whether that's possible from the beginning.

If the application depends on special technology that is difficult to source, that will also limit scale-up. Business process or function owners should discuss these scaling considerations with a company's IT organization before or during the pilot phase. An end run around IT is unlikely to be successful, even for relatively simple technologies like RPA. Integration with existing systems and processes was the greatest challenge organizations in the Deloitte "cognitive aware" survey encountered with the technology.

Full rollouts may also involve substantial change-management challenges. At one U.S. apparel retail chain, for example, the pilot project for what was expected to become a comprehensive AI implementation involved only a small subset of test stores. It incorporated machine learning for online product recommendations, predictions for optimal inventory and rapid replenishment models, and—most difficult of all—merchandising. Buyers, used to ordering product on the basis of their intuition, made comments like, "If you're going to trust this, what do you need me for?" After the pilot, the buyers went as a group to the chief merchandising officer and requested that the program be killed. To his credit, he pointed out that the results were positive and warranted expanding the project. He determined that buyers, freed of certain merchandising tasks, could take on more high-value work that humans can still do better than machines, such as understanding younger customers' desires and determining apparel manufacturers' future plans. But he realized that the buyers needed to be educated about a new way of working.

If scaling is to succeed, firms must also work to improve productivity. Cognitive technology may not result in savings from large layoffs anytime soon, but it does need to provide some business value. Many firms, for example, plan to grow their way into productivity—adding customers and transactions without adding staff. If headcount reduction is to be the primary factor justifying the investment, companies should ideally plan for those benefits to be realized over time through attrition or from elimination of outsourcing.

The Future Cognitive Company

The collection of consulting projects, the "cognitive aware" survey of managers, and interviews with companies suggest that managers who are experienced with AI are bullish on its prospects and moving ahead rapidly, if experimentally, with it. Although the early successes are relatively modest, I have no doubt that these technologies will eventually transform work. It seems likely that companies adopting these tools in moderation now—but that have aggressive implementation plans—will be as successful in their industries as those that embraced analytics early on.

Through the application of AI, information-intensive sectors such as marketing, healthcare, financial services, education, and professional services could become simultaneously more valuable and less expensive to society. The advice and recommendations they offer could be data-driven, could improve over time and with more data, and could be offered with little or no human intervention.

The execution and management of business drudgery in every industry and function—overseeing routine transactions, repeatedly answering the same questions, and extracting data from endless documents—could become the province of machines, freeing up human workers to be more productive and creative. Cognitive technologies are also the catalyst for making other data-intensive technologies succeed, including autonomous vehicles, the Internet of Things, and consumer technologies like mobile and multi-channel marketing.

There is no reason virtually every large company shouldn't be exploring cognitive technologies. Those who explore them earlier and more successfully, those who integrate AI with their business processes, and those who identify and nurture effective collaborations between humans and machines—those companies will dominate the future. They'll have more appealing products and services, more productive and effective processes, and people who have the time and freedom to be creative and resourceful on behalf of customers.

There will inevitably be some bumps in the road along the way to this future, and we need to keep our eyes looking far ahead for issues of workforce displacement (treated in chapter 6), technology challenges (chapter 7), and the organizational and social changes accompanying the use of smart machines (addressed in chapter 8). The application of AI to a large variety of business problems is clearly off and running.

4 What's Your Cognitive Strategy?

Artificial intelligence or cognitive technologies are burgeoning in the business world, but many companies are not yet getting strategic value from their projects and investments.[1] Their initiatives are not targeted at important business problems or opportunities. They may lack critical resources needed to achieve substantial projects. As one AI startup CEO put it, "AI has enormous promise but also a 1% problem. Less than 10 companies in the world are achieving the full potential of AI and the rest are really struggling."[2] This may be slightly exaggerated, but there is definitely truth to it.

A strategy for AI/cognitive technologies can help to address this problem. Some may question the value of a strategy for a specific technology, but it is warranted when the technology has significant potential to transform a business. Surveys of managers on cognitive technology bear out this potential significance. In a 2018 survey of senior executives in fifty large firms by NewVantage Partners, 72 percent of respondents named AI/cognitive technologies the disruptive technology they most expect to have an impact on their firms over the next decade—far higher than for any other technology. Respondents to the Deloitte "cognitive aware" survey that I have mentioned previously also ranked AI higher than any other technology in current importance.

If companies developed strategies for cognitive technology, it wouldn't be the first time that many did so for a specific technology. Many firms, for example, developed e-commerce strategies. More recently, *digital strategy*—a vague term, but one that includes a variety of ways to use information technology for business advantage—has been undertaken by many firms as well. Some firms also employed *big data* strategies to harness new data types and to develop the capabilities to analyze them.

Some may also feel that it is too early in the enterprise use of AI to create a full-blown strategy. But I know of many firms that have at least created aspects of an explicit strategy in some form of document, and many more who have answered—explicitly or implicitly—some strategic questions about their use of AI. So I would argue that it's not too early, and in any case, the strategic issues addressed in this chapter could easily inform an organization's thinking and posture on AI even if they're not ready for a fully articulated strategy.

One of the most important aspects of any strategy is how a key resource is going to affect your business. There are many potential choices for how cognitive technologies can change a company's strategy, products or business models—essentially the choice about how to use AI in your business. Strategies within companies or organizations are typically focused on two things: 1. What the organization sells or makes available to customers—its products and services; and 2. How it sells those offerings in the marketplace and makes money on them. In this chapter I'll describe both of these strategic elements in sections on products and business models. I'll also describe why, in many cases, AI hasn't really affected business models dramatically and how companies can make their AI work more strategic in nature.

There are also some key questions about how to build a strategy for AI and the necessary strategic capabilities to succeed. A section in this chapter describes the process for developing an AI strategy, and the key decisions relative to people who will build AI and the content of AI systems. I will also discuss just how ambitious an organization should be in its AI strategy. I'll end the chapter with a brief focus on how governments around the world are taking a strategic look at AI, and how that might influence businesses. Broader topics like technology strategies for AI and how to deal with organizational change management and issues are treated in separate chapters. In the next section we will turn to organizations that have surveyed executives to find out how they are thinking about the impact of AI on strategy.

The Strategic Impact of Cognitive Technologies

The 2017 survey by Deloitte of 250 "cognitive aware" executives found an extremely positive attitude toward cognitive technologies and their potential to drive change.[3] Eighty-eight percent of respondents in that survey agreed that cognitive technologies are either "important" or "very important" to product and service offerings, and even more—93 percent—agreed that they are important or very important to internal business processes. Although the technology is in its early stages of adoption, 83 percent said their companies have already achieved either moderate or substantial benefits from it. Seventy-six percent also believed that the technology would "substantially change" their companies within the next three years.

That survey also asked respondents their objectives for using cognitive capabilities in their business. Somewhat surprisingly, the most common response was to enhance existing products and services. More than half ranked that among the top three objectives. Creating new products and pursuing new markets also received a substantial level of support. "Reduce headcount through automation" was the least common response. All of the responses and the percentages selecting them (as first choice and then among the top three choices) are shown in figure 4.1.

Other surveys are also revealing about the strategic impact of cognitive technologies. A 2017 Genpact-sponsored survey of 300 global executives, for example, split respondents into "leaders" and "laggards" on benefits achieved from the technologies thus far.[4] In that survey, more than 40 percent of leaders said that AI improves the customer experience. Leaders were almost twice as likely to achieve increased revenues from AI (45 percent of leaders, compared to 25 percent of all respondents). When asked about their expectations three years from 2017, 87 percent of all respondents expect that AI will bring better customer experiences.

A Teradata survey of 260 senior executives from mid-to-large size organizations in the United States, Europe, and Asia found that the most common areas for driving revenue from AI investment were product

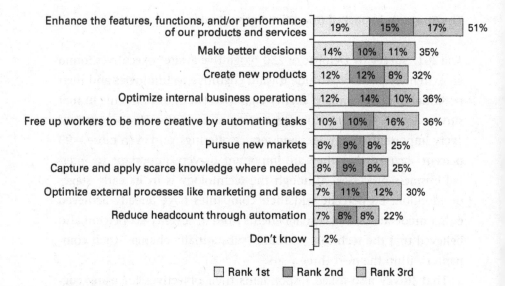

Figure 4.1
Benefits Sought from Cognitive Technologies
Source: 2017 Deloitte "Cognitive Aware" Survey

innovation/R&D (50 percent), customer service (46 percent), and supply chain and operations (42 percent). In terms of future investment, the primary business domains were customer experience (62 percent), product innovation (59 percent), and operational excellence (55 percent). Security and risk mitigation were also rated top priorities in both current and future investment.[5]

I mentioned the 2018 Gartner CIO survey in chapter 2, but a much smaller Gartner survey in July 2017 sheds light on the areas of the business to which cognitive technologies are being applied.[6] When eighty Gartner Research Circle members were asked about implementations in their organizations, the most common function (34 percent) was "customer engagement." A related area, "call center service/support" was second most common, with 29 percent, and "digital marketing" was third with 23 percent. The survey results also suggested that AI capabilities would be embedded within virtually all new software products by the year 2020.

A substantially larger McKinsey survey in 2017 had 3,000 global respondents, but similar to the other surveys, only 20 percent reported that their companies were using cognitive technologies "at scale."[7] That survey didn't address the areas of application for cognitive in detail but it notes that firms in the survey tended to adopt cognitive technologies affecting the "part of their value chain closest to the core." The authors give the example of the application of cognitive technologies to operations in such operationally intensive industries as automotive and assembly, consumer packaged goods, and utilities and resources. Operations and customer service were the most important areas for financial services firms. That is certainly a logical thing to do, and it's great that companies are being logical in their cognitive strategies.

The nature of the firm that conducts the survey may influence the results from it (not from distortion, but from the types of respondents surveyed and their concerns). TCS, a firm that does substantial work in IT operations and outsourcing, surveyed 835 large firms in 2017 about the areas to which they are applying cognitive technologies.[8] The top areas for application all involved IT:

Detecting and deterring security intrusions(44 percent)
Resolving users' technology problems (41 percent)
Reducing production management work by automating it (34 percent)
Gauging internal compliance in using approved tech vendors (34 percent)

Automating IT processes is undeniably important, but in most organizations it is a more tactical concern than improving products and services or relationships with customers. In the TCS survey, the most common application area outside of IT was "anticipating future customer purchases and presenting offers accordingly," with 19 percent.

A Problems/Issues/Opportunities Strategy

As these survey results suggest, one key decision that almost every organization faces with cognitive technology is where in the business to apply it. What business problems, issues, or opportunities can benefit from the use of cognitive technologies? Most businesspeople recognize that AI involves versions of knowledge, insight, and perception. But beyond that there are many specific decisions to be made about application.

Strategic thinking is, or at least should be, broad, high-level, and aspirational. So from an AI standpoint, the topics and examples in this chapter should have those attributes. However, as previous chapters have suggested, this is a bit of a problem with existing cognitive technologies. They perform relatively narrow tasks and primarily augment the work of human beings. So that generally means that they bring about incremental change, not transformational or disruptive change. And some of the "moon shot" AI projects that do involve highly strategic objectives—treating cancer, for example—have not always gone well. However, as I pointed out in the previous chapter, it is possible to aggregate a variety of shorter-term projects toward a larger, more strategic objective.

Internal or External Objectives?

Cognitive technologies can support so many different objectives that it's important to make strategic choices about which ones to emphasize. One key question is whether to focus on internal operations or external success with customers and products. Internal objectives might involve automating existing processes to cut costs, or optimizing internal decisions in functions like finance or supply chain management. Externally, a company might want to better understand and develop relationships with a particular type of customer, and use machine learning to analyze highly granular data on the customer. Or it might want to embed cognitive capabilities into a particular type of product.

This decision about the type of cognitive objectives to pursue should largely driven by business strategy. Verizon Wireless, for example, was beginning to experience small losses in revenue after many years of rapid growth. Its focus on cognitive technology was on externally oriented applications that lead to market growth—such as recommendations for new products and services, intelligent agents to increase customer satisfaction, and highly granular customer analysis to identify those most likely to spend more with the company.

A large European bank had a largely internally focused business strategy, which resulted in a different cognitive strategy. The company had a strong cost reduction orientation in a financial environment of very low interest rates. A major emphasis of its cognitive strategy was to support cost reduction through automation of jobs (mostly outsourced, but some internal as well) through robotic process automation. Wealth management was another long-term focus at the company, and it was working on cognitive technologies to support that emphasis. But given the cost reduction focus, the bank was attempting to develop a common technology approach for wealth management worldwide, rather than the decentralized approach by geographic region and client wealth levels that it had followed in the past.

Some firms have a multipronged focus with cognitive. GE has both an internal and external focus, with very different types of applications. Internally, a major usage of cognitive technology has been to apply machine learning to unify key data elements. I've mentioned this use of *probabilistic matching* across databases to create a unified supplier database. The technology could determine that "Acme Widgets Inc." at 123 Main St., Brooklyn, N.Y., was very likely to be the same firm as "Acme Inc." at "123 Main" in Brooklyn, and combine the two supplier records with little or no human intervention.

GE then moved on to customer and product data. In the customer domain, the company realized that some needed transformations in its sales approaches couldn't happen without an integration of its customer data. The company had over fifty different versions of its customer relationship management system. Even though they were all using Salesforce.com, they couldn't get an integrated perspective across the data in the systems. Using machine learning, GE integrated the data into a common Customer Hub; all the customer data from the different CRM systems is now unified in the hub. The project was finished in less than a year, and now salespeople can see what a customer is doing with GE all across the diversified company.[9]

Externally, I mentioned in the last chapter the GE "digital twin" approach to its digital/industrial strategy. That innovation enables predictive asset management on GE's industrial devices, and it's a good example of an external, product-oriented approach because it makes GE's products and services more desirable and distinctive in the marketplace.

Firms can also apply cognitive technology to advance external regulatory compliance and risk management objectives. This is particularly common in financial services firms. At NASDAQ (well known as a stock exchange, but also a financial information and software provider), for example, a key focus of cognitive initiatives has been on identifying potentially fraudulent or illegal financial trades and traders. Much of the company's efforts has been based on acquisitions or relationships with external cognitive startups. In 2015 it bought SMARTS, an Australia-based company that uses rules and machine learning to identify potentially problematic trades. And in 2017 it partnered with Digital Reasoning, a company that employs natural language processing, to identify communications among traders that might signal malfeasance. NASDAQ offers the combined capabilities from these two systems to other exchanges and to buyers and sellers of financial instruments.

Bank of New Zealand is one of many financial services companies that are employing cognitive technologies to fight financial crime and fraud. Financial crimes are amorphous and temporal by nature, so tools for identifying and fighting them should learn quickly and adapt to the ever-changing profile or malicious activities. They should augment human investigators and analysts by unifying intelligence from the vast and constantly growing amount of structured and unstructured data coming from systems of record, e-mails, and customer support tickets, as well as external sources.

Unfortunately most traditional crime detection approaches focus on structured data only and are based on rigid rules or rely on long model development and deployment cycles. This results in time gaps between initial crime and its discovery, leading to an endless loop of fraud–discovery–new fraud as crime schemes morph when identified. Another consequence is that existing legacy crime detection systems identify too many false positives that waste investigators' time and increase the risk of focusing on the wrong actors. A new approach is needed to zero in on the alerts that matter.

Bank of New Zealand (BNZ) is working in an early adopter program with Intel Saffron (an AI tool that Intel acquired in 2015), which has developed collaborative decision systems using associative memory AI to address this issue. The technology is grounded in identifying, counting, and analyzing associations across structured and unstructured data sets to highlight patterns, trends, anomalies, and similarities. The goal of the technology is to deliver a fast and transparent path to insight without requiring a preset model.

BNZ's investigators and analysts will use Intel Saffron to identify and prioritize anomalous activity based on risk scores. They will attempt to reduce the number of wrongly flagged customers or transactions and to accelerate the investigatory process and the accuracy of its outcomes. Offering a complete audit trail of the data used throughout the process, the system will also help the investigation teams address the increasing regulatory compliance challenge.

Customer-Focused Strategies

It's almost always a good idea to apply new technologies in ways that benefit customers. As I mentioned above, Verizon—specifically the Data Science and Cognitive Intelligence group, headed by Asim Tewary—focuses on applying analytics and cognitive technology to Verizon's interactions with customers. The group works closely, for example, with the company's marketing, digital operations, and customer care functions. Its strategic objective is to add increasing levels of intelligence to the company's marketing and customer service applications so that they ultimately pass the Turing Test—the long-standing but seldom realized objective that a user of an AI system would not be able to distinguish between it and a human. Verizon also has other internal groups that are focused on embedding AI capabilities in products, and on internal capabilities like the supply chain, but the customer focus is a strong one.

Capital One, the consumer-oriented bank that pioneered the use of many forms of analytics in banking, is now pursuing a variety of cognitive projects that have the ultimate potential of changing how people interact with their bank. It has undertaken a variety of AI projects that facilitate customer transactions, improve marketing, and help to prevent fraud.[10] As an initial foray, Capital One in 2016 became the first bank to allow access to customer accounts from the Amazon Alexa platform. In 2017 the bank announced the availability of Eno, a text-based chatbot allowing customers to check balances, pay bills, and do other simple transactions.

For its website, Capital One developed a machine learning application that allows it to customize site content based on the products and services the customer seems to be looking for. It also monitors fraud-oriented behavior, such as the length of time a user takes to enter security information.[11]

Capital One would also like to use sophisticated cognitive technologies—deep learning in particular—to make decisions at the heart of its business success, such as who should receive credit at what price.[12] However, the lack of algorithmic transparency in deep learning models currently means that regulators would not approve these methods. But Capital One is sufficiently devoted to strategic AI that it has formed a group to try to increase the level of transparency in these methods—an area of investigation generally reserved for academic researchers.

Verizon's attempt to beat the Turing Test, and Capital One's efforts to establish new frontiers in customer service, fraud, and credit decision-making, are clearly examples of customer-focused strategic initiatives. Each individual project these companies are pursuing may not be earth shattering, but together they will change how they go to market.

Making Better Internal Decisions

In terms of internally focused applications of AI, those focused on improving internal decisions are the most common. The role of cognitive technologies here—typically machine learning—is to enable decisions based on more detailed and faster-moving data. In many cases that means external data—which is welcome, because business decisions have long been based primarily on external data.

I will describe many examples of using machine learning for better internal decisions throughout this book. They include decisions related to marketing (personalized ads and offers), pricing, demand planning, operational planning, and even strategic planning.

For one detailed example, I'll describe the work of OpenMatters, a startup that uses AI and external data to classify and recommend business models. I'm on the board of this company, so I'm pretty familiar with it. The focus of the company is to analyze external company performance data and statements from company management in order to diagnose their business model (the four basic types are "assets and things," "people and services," "software and data," and "platforms and networks." Asset-intensive businesses have the lowest valuations; digital network orchestrators the highest. The founder, Barry Libert, has published multiple articles and books around the idea that different business models yield different corporate valuations.[13] The AI tool diagnoses what business model the company is in, and recommends steps the company might take to change or augment its business model. Libert has already used the tool in his own consulting, and has struck deals with several professional services firms for them to use it in their work with clients.

In a similar context, Boston Consulting Group has begun to quantify and analyze with machine learning tools the strategic orientations of companies, comparing them, for example, in terms of the need for large-scale transformation.[14] It is likely that we will see more consulting and professional services organizations employing such tools, and that they will eventually be adopted by client companies for their own ongoing use. These applications suggest that the impacts of AI on senior managers may ultimately be as great as that on front-line workers.

Developing New or Enhanced Product/Service Offerings

I was excited that many companies in the surveys mentioned earlier seem to be using cognitive technologies to develop new or enhanced product and service offerings. It's good news because it means that companies think they can make money or make their customers happy with cognitive capabilities. That in turn means that money and other resources will flow toward cognitive projects and senior executives will be more interested.

IT Products

We've been familiar with this product enhancement category in technology products for a while. Apple's Siri, Google's voice recognition, and Amazon's Alexa are all examples of adding cognitive speech recognition to product offerings, and they generally work quite well. Anyone using Google's Gmail or Inbox email applications will be familiar with the message classification and suggested replies that, respectively, preserve your attention and increase your productivity. We increasingly expect that our smartphones and apps will have such intelligence. These tools are likely to go well beyond their current functionality in the future to become "beachheads" in the home or office that gather, analyze, and add value to human activities—and help to make their providers richer and more successful.

Another example of a technology company with a largely product-focused approach to AI is Lenovo. The company has announced a series of cognitive technology–driven products that may be influential in the company's future product lines. They include: a context aware virtual assistant (CAVA) that uses facial recognition and natural language processing to make recommendations, SmartVest smart clothing that uses ten sensors and an ECG to monitor heart conditions; and the Xiaole platform, which is expected to "constantly learn from conversations with customers and adjust accordingly to provide a personalized and customized user experience." Certainly the specific products that eventually reach the marketplace will vary from these concepts, but they do bespeak a broad orientation by the company to embedding cognitive technology in their offerings.

As at Lenovo, most of the IT innovations from AI thus far have involved the user interface. But there are also developments involving the automated creation of the software programs that make technology work. This field goes under various names, such as code generation, metaprogramming, intentional programming, and model-based software engineering. It has been practiced at some level for a while, but has yet to make major inroads into the software development field. Thus far it has been used to increase the productivity of individual programmers, and to reduce the number of errors in the software they create. But there is no indication that it has eliminated programmers or even reduced the demand for them. However, I believe these developments will eventually call into question the idea that all students should learn computer programming.[15]

AI is also being used to automate or partially automate certain aspects of the software development process—that is, the creation of IT products—beyond basic programming. Software testing and quality assurance, for example, have been labor-intensive processes. But automated testing software can create thousands of test scripts in a few seconds that test many different uses of the software being tested. Again, however, this is creating only an incremental improvement in the overall speed and productivity of software development. These outcomes will probably increase and improve in an evolutionary fashion unless there is some dramatic AI breakthrough.

Plenty of evidence shows increasing numbers of software tasks can be directed and accomplished by nonprofessionals, and this will advance with cognitive technology assistance within IT products and services. Amateurs can already design websites, analyze data statistically, develop mobile apps, and even develop telecommunications networks with point-and-click interfaces and relatively few programming skills. Adding more intelligence to all kinds of programs will increase the roles that amateurs can play.

Finally, IT hardware products and architectures are also evolving to address the needs of AI and cognitive applications. Semiconductor firms, for example, are changing their architectures to speed AI-oriented computing. Firms are trying to emulate the success of Nvidia, whose graphics processing units (GPUs) were discovered to be well suited to deep learning applications, and whose financial fortunes have prospered greatly as a result. Chips are also being redesigned to handle the massive amounts of data that are produced in applications like autonomous vehicles.[16]

Product and Service Design

Software is also used to design products, and the field of product and service design is already evolving with the help of cognitive tools. *Generative design*, a new approach to computer-aided design, employs machine learning algorithms to translate high-level design goals and constraints into thousands of possible designs—most of which the human designer didn't anticipate. Autodesk is the most aggressive advocate of generative design, and is using it, for example, to help Airbus design a new light-weight cabin partition.[17] And for Autodesk, of course, this is an example of using cognitive capabilities to enhance an existing product.

Cognitive technology can even help service designers turn their high-level design thinking into products—at least if their products involve bits rather than atoms. At Airbnb, for example, the founders of the company have had a very strong design orientation (they met at the Rhode Island School of Design). New product/service design at Airbnb is typically very visually oriented; designers draw images on whiteboards, for example, to visualize key aspects of new offerings. Eventually, however, those hand-drawn designs have to be turned into code if they are going to be deployed on websites, in databases, and in online marketing campaigns.

In order to reduce the cycle time to get new products into the marketplace, Airbnb has developed an AI-based system that automatically translates informal design elements into code. Design technology lead Marcus Wilkins commented:

We've experimented using the same technology to live-code prototypes from whiteboard drawings, to translate high fidelity mocks into component specifications for our engineers, and to translate production code into design files for iteration by our designers.[18]

The company plans for AI-assisted prototyping to eventually be embedded in its product development software suite.

Non-IT Products and Services
We're beginning to see cognitive capabilities in product development or enhancement contexts outside of software and IT businesses as well. Since 2013, for example, Monsanto (which has been acquired by Bayer) has been offering *prescriptive planting* services for farmers that rely heavily on machine learning models of climate data, soil characteristics, and seed performance. Climate researchers can also use deep learning models to analyze satellite images. Monsanto had to spend roughly a billion dollars to get the climate data (from its acquisition of Climate Corporation for that price), but the machine learning models that analyze Climate's highly detailed and locale-specific weather data make it much easier for farmers to know when to plant, water, fertilize, harvest, and so

forth. Farmers pay for this advice, which is easier to justify when their crop yields increase by 10 to 15 percent—a typical improvement level. This approach is one component of "precision agriculture," which is expected to be necessary to feed the world's population.[19]

Another machine learning-based service that many companies are adding to their products today is *predictive maintenance* (sometimes called *predictive asset management*). I've already mentioned that service at GE, where it's a big part of the company's "digital industrial" push. But other industrial companies like Cummins Engine, Boeing, Caterpillar, and Robert Bosch are all using similar approaches. The data comes from sensors, and typically forms a time series of data. If companies can create labeled data that is associated with both healthy machines and those that have broken down, it's relatively easy to train models to identify when a machine is likely to break in the future. As industrial products become more reliable, some of these companies have had difficulty finding enough breakdown data to help their models predict it.

Entirely New Products

It is perhaps somewhat more difficult to use cognitive technologies to develop entirely new products than to enhance existing ones. That's particularly true in the pharmaceutical industry, where developing new drugs is extraordinarily time-consuming and expensive. To speed up that process and to try to make it more efficient, several pharma firms are trying to use cognitive technologies—IBM Watson in particular—to help develop new drugs.

One key reason for using Watson is that the average pharmaceutical researcher reads between 200 and 300 articles in a given year[20], while Watson for Drug Discovery has ingested 27 million Medline abstracts, more than 1 million full-text medical journal articles, and 4 million patents—and Watson is regularly updated. Watson for Drug Discovery can be augmented with an organization's private data, such as lab reports, and can help researchers look across disparate data sets to surface relationships and reveal hidden patterns through dynamic visualizations. None of these pharma firms is quite ready to declare victory in this drug development crusade, but executives in several firms do say that Watson has already helped to identify potential targets for drugs and has done so faster than it would have without the technology.

A related development is to use AI capabilities in products that determine whether a patient is taking the right drugs. Express Scripts, historically a major pharmacy benefits manager and distributor of prescription drugs, is adding new services and products that address that issue. The company offers a "drug utilization review" service to health insurers that evaluates new prescriptions for a patient relative to the other drugs the patient is taking. In the time that the patient is waiting for the prescription to be filled, the service can inform the pharmacist that the new drug is contraindicated with an existing prescription. The pharmacist can then discuss the potential problem with the patient.[21]

Express Scripts is also incorporating this type of capability into products. It is incorporating sensors and AI within an asthma inhaler that tracks a patient's usage of the device against his medical history to offer recommendations about more effective use of asthma medications.[22]

Another extension of the AI-based recommendation idea is to apply it to cosmetics and beauty aids. Procter & Gamble has used this approach to offer the Olay Skin Advisor app. It takes smartphone photographs of human (mostly female, presumably) faces and uses deep learning to analyze skin age and problem areas. It then recommends Olay skin care products that would be particularly well suited to the customer's skin.

New Business Models

Cognitive technologies can certainly support or drive strategic changes in business models. By "business models" I mean new ways to make money or serve customers; they include approaches to offering existing products and services, ways of going to market, distribution channels, and entering industries for companies beyond their existing ones.

New AI-Driven Business Models in the Automobile Industry

Perhaps the best examples today of established companies trying to change their business models with the help of AI are the automobile manufacturers Ford and General Motors. These companies were paragons of the industrial age, but they are seeking a new future based on electric vehicles, autonomous driving, and shared vehicles. Ford's new mission statement is "To become the world's most trusted mobility company by designing smart vehicles for a smart world."[23] GM isn't quite as aggressive in its objectives, but it too is trying to "translate breakthrough technologies into vehicles and experiences that people love." GM also wants to monetize some of the data generated by its almost nine million connected vehicles.

Both autonomous driving and shared vehicles depend heavily on AI capabilities (electric vehicles don't generally depend on them, although Toyota is apparently using AI to identify new materials for batteries or hydrogen fuel catalysts).[24] The need for AI in autonomous vehicles is well known. It perceives the road and any obstacles in it, and makes decisions about how and where to drive. I won't enter the debate here about when fully autonomous vehicles will be widely available, although I tend to think it will be longer than many Silicon Valley proponents predict. But there is little doubt that strong AI capabilities are necessary for autonomy to be realized. Ford and GM have acquired autonomous driving companies (Argo AI by Ford, Cruise Automation by GM), and invested or partnered with various other companies. Both companies have established Silicon Valley outposts with many AI researchers.

Vehicle sharing is also data and AI-intensive—at least in companies like Uber and Lyft. At Lyft, for example, machine learning is used to some degree in the company's routing, pricing, and driver matching algorithms,[25] and the first two would continue in autonomous shared rides. Uber has created a broad "machine learning as a service" platform that furnishes model-based predictions to a variety of Uber services across the company.[26] Uber says that it uses machine learning "among other areas ... to enable an efficient ride-sharing marketplace, identify suspicious or fraudulent accounts, suggest optimal pickup and dropoff points, and even facilitate more delicious UberEATS delivery by recommending restaurants and predicting wait times so your food can get to you when you need it."[27]

It's not yet clear, of course, whether Ford and GM can compete effectively with AI-centric companies like Alphabet's Waymo, and Uber and Lyft from the ride-sharing industry. Both auto manufacturers have upgraded their analytics capabilities over the past several years and brought in chief data and analytics officers from outside. Acquiring the necessary AI talent, competing with established players in the ride-sharing industry, and solving the enormous technical challenges of autonomous driving would be difficult for any firm. If they do become "smart mobility" companies, however, it's clear that AI will have a lot to do with it.

Startups and the Persistence of Established Business Models

Most of the other companies that are attempting to create AI-driven business models are startups, which have the advantage of having no previous business model to change or disrupt. However, even they run into challenges when they take their new business models to market.

One example of this is in the medical imaging (radiology) industry, where "computer-aided diagnosis" has been discussed for decades but has thus far failed to yield much change in the cost or business model for medical imaging. As I argued in chapter 2, this is despite substantial progress in using deep learning to identify potential problems in images. Several startups (as well as some big companies like IBM) are claiming that very soon it will be commonplace to employ AI-diagnosed imaging in medical practice.

For example, Enlitic, a San Francisco-based company that applies deep learning to radiology images, suggests that it has already well underway with this business model. Its website, for example, says:

Deep learning is a technology inspired by the workings of the human brain. Networks of artificial neurons analyze large datasets to automatically discover underlying patterns, without human intervention. Enlitic's deep learning networks examine millions of images to automatically learn to identify disease. Unlike traditional Computer Aided Diagnostics (CAD), deep learning networks can scout for many diseases at once. They can also provide rich insights in areas such as early detection, treatment planning, and disease monitoring.[28]

However, you won't find many (or any on my search) mentions of hospitals or radiology practices actually using Enlitic's solution, because introducing radiology "without human intervention" into clinical care is a difficult business model.

To find out why, I interviewed Dr. Keith Dreyer, who is a radiologist and chief data science officer at Partners Healthcare, a large academic medical center in Boston. Dreyer is positive about the implications of deep learning for radiology:

We've had CAD for a couple of decades, but deep learning is a much better technology. It will provide much higher sensitivity and specificity than we have today, and radiologists will trust it. Integrating it with clinical practice offers many potential benefits.

However, the "without human intervention" business model isn't quite ready for prime time, as he notes:

The American College of Radiology [a professional association of which Dreyer is on the Board of Chancellors] created the Data Science Institute [ACRDSI] this past spring. In conjunction with the CCDS, the ACR Data Science Institute did an analysis of several FDA-approved pulmonary nodule detectors. They were all based on deep learning. We were interested in whether they provided similar numbers, and how they compared to each other. But none of their outputs were the same! Some focused on the probability of a lesion, others the probability of cancer. Some would describe the features inside a nodule, some would give its location. So we concluded at the ACR that we needed to define the inputs and outputs for the vendors of these machines. We need to be able to verify the algorithms before and after they are taken to market in terms of their effectiveness and value. We need to develop some initial processes for radiologists to use. We will need to have a "saliency map" for why the system says cancer, and ideally we'll have things like reason codes to aid with transparency.

Although deep learning technology is developing rapidly in research labs like those at Enlitic (and at one within Partners Healthcare—the Center for Clinical Data Science, with which Dreyer is affiliated), it's pretty clear that working out the details of its use in practice will take many years. It will also require the combined efforts of startups like Enlitic, big companies like IBM and GE, hospital networks like Partners, health insurance companies and government payers, and professional associations like the ACR, to make this new business model a reality.

Even AI-centric business models that incorporate human augmentation can be difficult to launch and scale. In the travel agency industry, for example, Paul English, a co-founder of the online agent Kayak, has founded a new company called Lola that incorporates both human and machine-driven help to travelers. English describes the machine component:

Our code generates an algorithm for every single traveler based on their click stream and their purchase history. The algorithm learns what [the traveler] likes and will surface those results to the user. We also do user clustering and similarity models so that when a traveler doesn't have a history of going to, say, Miami, we can still surface a hotel choice that is relevant to them. We look at things like price history and sentiment data. We parse millions of reviews [to determine] which words provide key information about the types of hotels the traveler likes. For example, I like the Gansevoort hotel in New York, so [Lola] would find hotels with similar key words and sentiment data on a hotel in Miami.[29]

But in addition to these AI-based recommendations, Lola also has a group of human travel agents that can help with the details of travel. The agents, who usually communicate with customers via text messages, can handle details of travel that automated systems usually overlook: overall planning of trips, early arrival or late checkout at hotels, room upgrades, and dealing with unexpected weather events.

This business model seems like a good idea, but Lola has thus far had challenges finding its niche in the crowded travel agency marketplace. The company began as a service for leisure travelers, but now is focusing on business travelers from small to midsize businesses, as they do not face the same limitations that business travelers from large corporations or leisure travelers do. Business travelers from large corporations face restrictions in the fares they can book, and leisure travelers are often looking for the lowest fares from online sites like Kayak.

Why Existing Business Models Persist in the Face of AI

The same comments about the radiology and travel agency industries might be applied to a variety of other industries and business domains. AI startups tout their ability to reshape the legal industry, the trucking industry, the retail industry, the financial services industry, and many others. But conventional business models stubbornly persist. What are the factors that keep existing models in place? An understanding of them will make it possible for us to better understand when cognitive technologies will actually drive change in business models. Here, then, are nine factors that limit AI-driven business model change:

1. *Technologies aren't quite there yet*—Many cognitive technologies are close to being good enough to change business models, but aren't quite there yet. Autonomous vehicles, for example, can handle many or most driving situations, but not all of them. Being able to negotiate situations like snow and rain, unpredictable pedestrians, difficult intersections, and so forth always seems to be tantalizingly on the horizon.

2. *Partial solutions are all that's available*—Cognitive technologies can automate tasks, but not entire jobs. Since they usually can't replace entire employees, they don't offer high levels of economic benefit, and they are adopted slowly. In legal applications, for example, cognitive tools can largely automate such tasks as legal research in a few domains of law, rapid review of documents, and extraction of contract provisions. But these are either narrow tasks or are performed by relatively low-paid employees. They haven't had a major impact on law firms for this reason.

3. *AI picks off the easiest parts of the process*—In industries in which cognitive technologies have gathered significant adoption, they have used AI to address the easiest parts of the problem. Providing "robo-advice" in financial services is a good example. In those applications, advisory firms use AI—at least a relatively primitive form of machine learning—to do asset allocation of mutual funds and exchange traded funds. But that is the easy part of investing advice. Much more difficult problems involve learning from investing behavior, managing a broad range of asset classes, and financial activities beyond retirement investing. Robo-advisors may take those on at some point, but until then they won't provide much of a threat to the conventional advising business model.

4. *No common sense*—Cognitive technologies aren't yet capable of common sense despite several decades of trying, although there may finally be some progress in that regard.[30] Until they can, solutions based on AI will fall short in some respects. For example, in medical diagnosis, there is a tendency for cognitive solutions (specifically

IBM's Watson—perhaps the most medically focused of all market offerings) to identify rare and complex diseases as the cause of symptoms—even though such a diagnosis is much less probable than with a more commonly encountered disease. This lack of "diagnostic parsimony" can lower physicians' faith in AI's credibility and make them unlikely to adopt it for routine medical practice.[31]

5. *Startup processes are required, but startups don't have the customers*— Radically different business models require radically different business processes, designed from scratch to be substantially more efficient or effective. But even if startups designed such processes, they'd have challenges successfully acquiring customers for them. In radiology, for example, not only radiologists would need to agree to new processes, but also hospitals, patients, and insurance companies.

6. *Big companies buy the startups*—Even when emerging vendors of cognitive technologies have promising solutions that could revolutionize business models, they are often acquired by larger companies, which tend to move more slowly in deploying them. In the *fintech*—new technology startups for the financial services industry—sector, many observers felt that major changes to business models were on the way. Instead, however, banks have begun to acquire or make substantial equity investments in fintech startups, and the pace of change from AI and other emerging technologies has slowed.[32]

7. *Startups don't have the resources to wait out the change*—Startups typically have limited resources, and they may not be sufficient to fund the company until it reaches a "critical mass" phase of adoption. At the moment there is substantial venture and private equity capital available for AI startups, but it won't last forever. Any overall downturn in the technology company environment is likely to be punishing on AI startups as well, and on their ability to wait out new business models.

8. *The installed base will take a while to disappear*—In several industries that are affected by cognitive technologies, there is a large installed

base that will take many years to depart from the scene. For example, in the case of autonomous cars and trucks, there are many non-autonomous vehicles that will be on the roads for decades. Unless governments or insurance companies decide to reward drivers for shifting to autonomous vehicles, the adoption of these new technologies will be slow. There is also often a difficult technical challenge when autonomous vehicles have to deal with human-driven vehicles on the same roads.

9. *Most cognitive applications are standalone, but need integration*—Many of the cognitive solutions thus far offered in the marketplace solve a relatively isolated problem, and they are standalone solutions. However, in order to be effectively deployed in large organizations, they need to be something other than standalone, that is, integrated with existing systems and processes. If, for example, a company wants to qualify its sales lead stream by digging up and integrating external information on that company (through some combination of machine learning and natural language processing), it will need either to force its salespeople to learn a new system, or to integrate it with its customer relationship management (CRM) system. An alternative, of course, would be to buy such capabilities from an established CRM vendor; Salesforce.com, for example, has some AI capabilities called Einstein that are integrated with transactional capabilities. Of course, Salesforce acquired many of those capabilities from startups.

The Objectives and Processes of a Cognitive Strategy

As with most strategies, the goal of cognitive strategy is to surface, answer, and achieve consensus on key questions as an organization. As I've noted above, many important decisions are to be made about cognitive technology, and without a strategy—or at least some serious deliberation on strategic questions—they may be made in a haphazard or ineffective manner. Firms can waste money and time on cognitive technology with a poor or nonexistent strategy.

There may or may not be people within a company who are capable of developing a cognitive strategy. Candidates should have the following traits:

• They should know something about the major types of cognitive technology and how they are used in business
• They should be effective at communicating to managers in nontechnical terms
• They must understand the key issues of the business and its current strategic direction
• As with other types of strategy development, facilitation and process skills would also be useful

If potential cognitive strategists don't have some of the required knowledge, they may be able to obtain it through interviews. And as with other strategies, there are external consultants who can assist in the process. If a firm employs external experts, however, it's still important to engage the internal management team in the process and the outcome.

Firms use a variety of approaches to set strategy, but cognitive strategy should be collaborative and should involve at least some degree of process.[33] A unilateral approach by the CEO is unlikely to engage the organization, and an entirely ad hoc approach is unlikely to yield a rigorous and evidence-based result. The process should include interviews with internal and external experts, workshops, and strategy review sessions.

The goal of the process should not be to develop a strategy document, but to drive educated and informed actions. In many cases, the outcome of an effective strategy will be a series of pilots, proofs of concept, or production deployments of cognitive tools in various parts of the business.

Strategizing about cognitive technologies is complicated by the fact that many managers do not understand the different technologies and what can be done with them. It may, then, be helpful to conduct some sort of management education program prior to a strategy effort.

The remainder of this chapter primarily addresses the specific topics or substrategies on which the organization needs to take a position relative to cognitive technology. Of course, the specific topics an organization addresses may vary, and can itself be the focus of the early stages of a strategy process.

A Content Strategy

Cognitive technology is primarily about analyzing and extracting insights from content—data, information, or knowledge. An important strategic component is to determine what type of content a company will be using in its cognitive projects. Ideally a company would have some proprietary or exclusive content that it could use in its own products and processes. If the content is unstructured (textual, for example), that knowledge must be codified and structured in some fashion so that it can be used in a cognitive system. This problem is most critical in semantically oriented natural language processing applications, which I described in chapter 1. Machine learning applications using structured numeric data don't typically need as much content structuring, but they do require a lot of data.

Put another way, what type of knowledge graph does the company want to own? A knowledge graph is a set of entities (people, places, objects) and facts about them and their relationships. Google pioneered the idea of the knowledge graph with a collection of billions of facts about search entities. LinkedIn is another company with a proprietary knowledge graph; it consists of facts about members, their job titles, companies worked for, educations, locations, and so forth.

Some firms obtain their knowledge graphs from vendors. IBM's Watson business, for example, bought content about medical images when it acquired Merge Healthcare in 2013, and also gets additional images from a collaborative it formed of a number of medical centers and radiological image providers. It makes the knowledge graph derived from those images available to its Watson Health customers—for a price, of course.

Watson is also well known for "ingesting" textual content, such as that in medical journals, and making it available to answer questions. But less well known is that a considerable amount of effort often needs to be put into structuring that content into "question/answer pairs" that can be used in interactions with clinicians. This can require considerable input and time from experts.

Some vendors of cognitive software may insist on licensing agreements that the knowledge graph resulting from a particular application of the software is owned (or co-owned) by the vendor. Several companies I have interviewed have decided not to use certain vendors because of these restrictive intellectual property agreements.

It stands to reason, for example, that a company should be reluctant to turn over ownership and usage rights to its customer and product information, or to proprietary process information, to some other organization—even if that organization can add significant value to it. Such information should be viewed as a valuable corporate asset, and firms should find ways to add value to it themselves as a key aspect of corporate strategy.

"User" (rather than vendor) companies with no intention of selling access to their knowledge graph often obtain some of it from vendors, but have to undertake the "last mile" of customization on their own, or with the vendor's consultants. Take, for example, an insurance company that wants to build an "intelligent agent" for customer interactions. It might contract with IBM Watson, IPsoft Amelia, or some other provider for the basic English (or Swedish or Italian) language knowledge graph or dialog graph. But the vendor probably will not have developed the graph to include all the language and taxonomies related to the insurer's specific products and processes, so that will have to be developed before implementation is successful. As one manager of cognitive technologies working on such an intelligent agent at a life insurance company put it in an interview:

We need to learn the customer's intention, but in order to do that you have to incorporate some old-fashioned knowledge engineering. The knowledge engineer has to develop ontologies, cases, and text classifications to put each interaction into an intention—a node in the dialog graph. If the customer's true intention falls outside of the one we have inferred, the system just seems stupid. It's critical to realize—on our part and the customer's part—that the domain of discussion is very limited. If you know that in advance and your expectations aren't too high, you can have a great outcome.

A Talent Strategy

A key question for any organization pursuing cognitive initiatives is where to get people who can do such work. This is, of course, an extension of the previous challenge that organizations had in securing qualified quantitative analysts, and then data scientists. The good news is that since these challenges surfaced, universities (more than 400 of them in the United States alone) have been churning out large numbers of graduates who are broadly educated in analytics and data science. The bad news is that they have probably not been trained in cognitive technologies and methods in particular. Few university faculty are familiar enough with these technologies to teach about some of them; those who are have probably been hired away from universities into tech companies over the last several years.

Estimates about the number of well-trained, experienced AI practitioners vary widely, although no one seems to believe there are enough. Element AI, a Montreal-based AI startup, has done several estimates of the number of qualified AI people in the world, with different versions of "qualified." That company's estimates range from 5,000 to 90,000, but they assume that a PhD is necessary—to me, a highly questionable assumption. The China-based firm TenCent estimated that there are between 200,000 and 300,000 AI experts and trained practitioners globally.[34] In any case, most firms find it difficult to source the AI talent that they feel they need.

The choices for talent strategy are similar to those for other specialized experts: buy, build, or rent. To buy people is to hire those who already possess the needed skills. This will be particularly difficult if your company is not in New York, Boston, or the San Francisco Bay area, and it is not willing to pay large compensation figures, including stock options. It will also be important to such individuals that you have plenty of data to work with and that your organization is undertaking some interesting challenges in the field.

To build people is to train them in the needed skills. This will be much less difficult if the candidates for such training already have basic analytical and data management skills. Machine learning, in particular, is an automated form of analytics, albeit with a wide variety of algorithms to choose from. To do it well, employees would need to know something about the underlying algorithms, what data are well suited to machine learning, and how to go about "feature engineering," or the manipulation of variables and their transformations in models to achieve a good fit with the data. If the training is on semantic-type applications (as with some forms of natural language processing), the precursor education and experience should revolve around "computational linguistics"—the use of computer applications to do semantic forms of NLP.

It is relatively rare for companies to engage in substantial efforts to train or retrain their employees in data science and cognitive skills, but it should be more common. One company that has done it is Cisco Systems. That company created a distance learning program for aspiring data scientists with two different universities. The program lasts for nine months and concludes with a certificate in data science from the university. Several hundred data scientists have been trained and certified, and are now based in a variety of different functions and business units at Cisco. In addition, the company created a two-day executive program led by business school professors on what analytics, data science, and cognitive technologies are and how they are typically applied to business problems. The program also covers how to manage a workforce that includes data scientists, and how to know whether their outputs are effective.

A third option is to "rent" a cognitive-informed workforce, which is to hire consultants or vendors to deliver services. This strategy is widely practiced by firms that don't have the in-house expertise to build cognitive applications. It can be successful if the vendor or consulting firm has sufficiently well trained people (although they also suffer from the shortage and some may inflate credentials). If a firm is interested in building longer-term capabilities in the cognitive space, it should staff projects with a mixture of rented people and its own employees.

A fourth option, which can be combined with the others I have described, is to rely more heavily on technology that can augment the efforts of amateur AI practitioners, sometimes called *citizen data scientists.* One technology that does so is automated machine learning technology, which is offered by firms like DataRobot (a Boston-based firm to which I am an advisor), SAS Viya (in the Autotune function), and Google (in the form of AutoML, which is in "alpha test" as I write).

With DataRobot, the technology does fundamental data cleaning, addresses missing data, and then undertakes a contest among as many as a hundred different algorithms to determine which is most effective at predicting the chosen outcome. The company often describes a *ballerina*—technically an associate at a large bank with an undergraduate degree in sociology and a love for ballet—who is able to create some highly profitable new trading models with the aid of automated machine learning. Another account in an insurance company describes a positive outcome from DataRobot's technology:

[Scot] Barton [head of an R&D group at Farmers Insurance] first tried using the platform by inputting a bunch of insurance data to see if it could predict a specific dollar value. Compared with a standard, hand-built statistical approach, the model selected had a 20 percent lower error rate. "Out of the box, with the push of one button; that's pretty impressive," he says.[35]

Some question whether amateurs will get into trouble with such machine learning automation, perhaps "overfitting" models by using too many predictive variables, or violating statistical assumptions. But I have not heard of any real problems with this in the several companies I have spoken with about their use of the technology.

Another company has employed automated machine learning tools as part of a structured effort to embed advanced machine learning methods throughout their organization—in fact, the effort is called Embed Machine Learning, or EML. The project is at 84.51°, a company wholly owned by Kroger that does analytical and AI projects for the retailer and its suppliers. The number in the name is the longitude of Cincinnati; the company is based there and works with longitudinal data.

EML, headed by Scott Crawford, is a formal mission to enable, empower, and engage the organization to better use and embed machine learning. "Enable" meant providing the infrastructure to efficiently use and embed machine learning such as the servers, software, and data connectivity. "Empower" involved identification of the best set of machine learning tools and training analysts and data scientists to use those tools. After evaluating more than fifty tools, 84.51° selected R, Python, and Julia as its preferred machine learning languages, and settled on DataRobot's automated machine learning platform as its primary software environment. "Engage" meant motivating internal clients to use the tools by demonstrating and socializing the benefits through several proofs of concept, advancing code sharing/examples (via Github), and consulting.

Another part of the EML initiative was to develop a standard methodology for machine learning use. Its internally developed methodology, which it calls 8PML (84.51° Process for Machine Learning), is unusual within nonvendor organizations. Most machine learning effort in companies is focused on development of models, but 84.51° was interested in a broader focus. 8PML begins with the Solution Engineering phase, in which the analysis is framed, and the business objectives for the project are clarified and compared to available resources. For example, a project's business objective might require a very large number of models to be routinely updated and quickly deployed, without the requisite budget and staffing. Automated machine learning technology can lower the amount of resources required and can change the "art of the possible" given its ability to rapidly fit, update, and deploy thousands of predictive models.

In the Model Development phase of the methodology, data are analyzed, variables or features are engineered, and the model that best fits the training data is identified. Automated machine learning speeds this phase of the process considerably, increasing the productivity of data scientists. That frees them up to fit more models and/or to give more effort to other high value aspects of the process (e.g., solution engineering and feature engineering). The technology also makes it possible for less skilled practitioners to generate high-quality models. Detailed knowledge of which algorithms are appropriate for certain analyses is no longer essential; automated machine learning takes over that function.

The third and final component of the 84.51° approach to machine learning is Model Deployment, in which the chosen model is deployed in production systems and processes. Given the scale of machine learning applications at Kroger—the sales forecasting application, for example, creates forecasts for each item in each of more than 2,500 stores for each of the subsequent fourteen days—this stage of the process is key.

Many companies today are experimenting with machine learning, but 84.51° and Kroger have taken this AI approach to the next level. The Embedded Machine Learning initiative, standardizing on an automated machine learning tool, and the three-stage machine learning methodology have all helped to create a "machine learning machine." Models are framed, developed, and deployed in the same way that a well-managed manufacturing organization might create physical products. We'll probably see multiple examples of this factory-like approach to machine learning in the future, but 84.51° is practicing it today.

I should also point out that the people who are building cognitive applications—and the development processes they employ—are not the only important aspect of a talent strategy. People are also needed who have business analysis skills and can frame the business problem to be solved and do a high-level translation into what technologies might address it. This "translator" function is critical to success with AI, and it requires only a rudimentary understanding of how cognitive technologies function. In addition, executives and managers who understand the value and purposes for cognitive technologies can "pull" them into their functions and processes. This can rarely be done successfully as a "push" from technologists.

A Partnering or Acquisition Strategy

Most companies choose to build and deploy cognitive technologies on their own, using their own people—or perhaps they get some help from consultants or vendors. However, it's not uncommon these days to partner with or acquire companies that can provide a significant head start in AI capabilities.

Given the scarcity of people with significant AI expertise, an acquisition can be a rapid means of bringing in a cadre of smart folks. Some startups or partners may possess proprietary data, software, or algorithms that can be of value to a company needing those assets.

The acquisition approach is particularly common among IT vendors, who have bought many AI-related startups. Perhaps the king of acquisitions is Google, which has bought 12 AI-related firms since 2012—including DeepMind, which it seems to be relying upon heavily in its AI research and product development. Apple, Microsoft, Facebook, Twitter, Intel, Baidu, and Salesforce have bought multiple AI firms.[36]

The other industry whose members have decided that they need a lot of AI capabilities quickly is the auto manufacturing sector. General Motors, for example, bought the autonomous vehicle firm Cruise Automation, which has a strong AI focus. Ford bought Argo AI for a billion dollars. Both companies are rapidly adding employees to the newly acquired business units, which have been kept largely separate from their parent companies. GM says that it will increase Cruise Automation's employee count in San Francisco from forty-six when the company was acquired to over 1,600 by 2021.[37] It is relying heavily on Cruise to develop software for making its electric Chevrolet Bolt car self-driving for ride sharing applications.

Some firms—particularly those in the auto and mobility industry, have relied heavily on partnerships rather than acquisitions. Many, for example, have partnered with Waymo, the Alphabet business unit that has been working on autonomous driving longer than any other firm. Among the firms that have partnered with Waymo are Fiat Chrysler, Avis, Intel, Lyft, AutoNation, and the insurance firm Trov. The semiconductor firm Nvidia, which makes processors well-suited to AI-based image recognition, has also partnered with many firms in the auto industry.[38] The overall number of partnerships for advancing autonomous vehicles is somewhat dizzying. Of course, partnerships can be fragile and fleeting, and it is too early to say whether partnerships or acquisitions are a more effective route to self-driving cars.

An Ambition Strategy

The last strategic component I will discuss is just how ambitious an organization should be with regard to its cognitive technology projects. As I mentioned at the beginning of chapter 1, some organizations pursue highly ambitious moon shots like treating cancer or reinventing customer relationships. Others have more modest ambitions, like adding an intelligent agent as a new, experimental channel to customers, or automating an existing set of tasks with RPA.

There is no right answer to the question of how much ambition is appropriate. However, there are relatively few examples of radical transformation with cognitive technologies actually succeeding, and many examples of "low hanging fruit" being successfully picked.

My advice for most firms would be to develop a series of less ambitious applications that are in the same area of the business (say, all involving customer relationships and interactions) and that in combination have a substantial effect on the business. That way each individual project can be low-risk, and the company will have time to ease its way into a transformation.

Say, for example, your automobile insurance company wants to transform its claims processes for customers' accidents. A moon shot would be one AI application that evaluates a claim for automobile damage—perhaps submitted by a customer photograph from a smartphone—and determines the cost to fix it, instantly paying the amount into the customer's bank account. But needless to say, this would be very difficult.

Less ambitious but still quite useful steps in this direction might involve, for example, a deep learning project to evaluate multiple photos sent in by a body shop to determine whether there is frame damage to the car or not. At the same time, a company could work on an application to question customers about a claim and recommend the best place to fix the car. It might also work on a machine learning program to evaluate the possibility of a fraudulent claim.

There is, of course, a case for cognitive transformation in a single moon shot project, but the circumstances under which this is reasonable are somewhat rare. It should involve technology that is mature and tested. It should be adopted within an organization that has a lot of AI experience, one that has already had success with large-scale IT-driven transformation, and one in which senior managers are fully on board with the initiative. The organization should be good at—and prepared for—substantial process and behavior change. It should be willing to tolerate a high level of risk. If all of those circumstances are present, a moon shot may be viable.

Given all the media and vendor hype in the cognitive technology space, companies often feel pressure from senior managers or boards of directors to take on a cognitive project, sometimes at the urging of a particular vendor. Some firms have already made mistakes in terms of the technologies or consultants selected for their projects. It's much better for a company to try to see beyond marketing blandishments about AI and to create the best fit with the organization's strategy, business model, and capabilities.

Country-Based AI Strategies

The primary focus for strategic thinking about cognitive technologies has been within private companies. But government bodies—particularly countries—have been getting in on the game as well. They are establishing priorities for research and development, providing funding for research and startups, and developing AI talent strategies. Businesses based in particular countries can either benefit or suffer from the amount of activity undertaken by governments, especially when the governmental initiatives are collaborative with businesses. If the government where your business—or a part of it—is based is supporting business-oriented AI research, chances are good that many companies will benefit from it.

The largest government-backed AI initiatives on the planet are in China. The country has announced a multibillion-dollar initiative to become the world leader in AI by 2030. This is the largest monetary commitment to AI in the world from a government. One Chinese state alone has said it will devote $5 billion to developing AI technologies and businesses. These government programs will support ambitious moon-shot projects, start-ups, and academic research in AI. The program will also address the role of AI in China's defense and intelligence industries.[39] Chinese online firms also have massive amounts of data on which to train machine learning algorithms. The wild card for China is whether the government will use AI for social control in ways that make world-class AI experts less interested in working and living there.[40]

At the other extreme from China in size, one of the most active countries in AI implementation is Singapore, which often takes the lead among countries in strategizing about new technologies. The city state is clearly very serious about building its AI capabilities, and has announced the following initiatives:

• AI is the most prominent technology in the country's latest Industry Transformation Map for its critical information, communications, and media industry sector. The map encompasses such steps as developing a "National Speech Corpus" of audio and text files to help organizations understand local speech and accents, co-funding the development of AI projects in companies, and a program for small to medium enterprises to help them identify AI applications in their businesses.

• Singapore's National Research Foundation is investing over $100M US over five years to enhance adoption of AI to solve business problems, and will support 100 AI experiments in local companies.

• The country has created an AI apprenticeship program to create 200 trained professionals over the next three years.

• The government is partnering with several technology companies to assist them in adding AI capabilities to products that are made in Singapore.

• Singapore's Government Technology Agency has sponsored a program called Smart Nation that harnesses AI, data analytics, and the Internet of Things to address key problems in the country.[41]

Some might argue that it is easier for a small country like Singapore to mobilize around an idea like artificial intelligence, but the resolve and resources that the country is applying to the technology are clearly impressive. And it sets a good example for other nations.

Some other countries, while perhaps not as ambitious as China or Singapore in the size or breadth of their efforts, are also establishing strategies and programs involving AI:

• The U.K.'s latest budget includes £75 million for AI, including funding for startups, for PhD students in U.K. universities, and for an advisory board to identify and help to remove barriers to AI development in the country.[42] The U.K. was ranked first in an index of "AI Readiness" by the research firm Oxford Insights; the index employs criteria such as public service reform, economy and skills, and the availability and quality of public data.[43] However, there is no evidence yet that these traits will generate strong AI capabilities over time.

• Ireland's Irish Development Authority has attempted to facilitate the development of an AI company ecosystem, and the government is also funding a masters program in AI.[44]

• The Canadian Institute for Advanced Research received $125M Canadian in government funding to support education and research in AI, building on the country's early lead in deep learning research.[45]

Meanwhile, the United States is doing relatively little in terms of government strategy. The Obama administration did commission two reports setting direction with regard to AI at the end of his term, and they argued for making the technology an urgent priority.[46] And the country ranked second in the "Government AI Readiness Index."

However, the Trump administration appears to care little about AI or any other technology. Treasury Secretary Stephen Mnuchin, when asked about the impact of AI on jobs, said that, "It's not even on our radar screen," and that significant job loss from AI is "50 to 100 years away."[47] The administration has attempted to cut research funding in general and has proposed no major government programs related to AI. As a result, of course, the United States is likely to fall behind other countries in the race to develop and commercialize AI.

Fortunately the United States does have a strong private sector effort in this technology. In 2015, for example, the combined R&D spending at Google, Apple, Facebook, IBM, Microsoft, and Amazon was $54 billion— more than the R&D spending of the U.K. government.[48] Much of that spending went toward AI research. It makes for an interesting experiment to see whether private or public sector efforts to advance AI prove to be more effective.

Making Strategic Progress

Some organizations may not be ready for a full strategy, but they should at least consider some of the questions in this chapter. A company that wants to adopt AI in its business will be much more successful if it has some deliberations up front about where it should apply the technology, what objectives to try to achieve, how it will source the talent, and so forth.

Management teams all over the world are beginning to ask themselves what they should be doing with these technologies. It's important not to be overly swayed by vendor or consultant marketing, and to have an in-depth discussion about what AI capabilities make sense for your business. Even if your approach involves only a pilot or proof of concept, you don't want to get started on the wrong foot—or technology—if you can help it through some strategic analysis.

At some point, as AI technologies become mainstream, strategic discussions about them can be integrated with those about other technologies. For now, however, the technologies are different enough, and their implications for business processes and employee jobs significant enough, that they should probably be considered on their own.

5 AI Tasks, Organizational Structures, and Business Processes

What would you do with a machine that could see—perceive images and determine what they are? Or how would you redesign a business activity if you had a machine that met the Turing Test—one that could converse via speech or text with a human being, and the human couldn't tell whether the conversation is with another human or a machine? What if your machine could find unexpected patterns in any dataset? How would machines that can do virtually any structured, specifiable task without (much) human intervention change your organization?

This is the situation faced by designers of organizational processes and structures in the age of smart machines. The capabilities I've described are either already available, or are just around the corner. Astute businesspeople therefore need to be aware of what these intelligent devices can do, and how they can incorporate them into their organization and its work. That's the focus of this chapter.

In keeping with the "real world" orientation of this book, my focus is not so much on what AI will be able to do in the distant future, but on what it can do today and in the very near future. For example, as I've already noted several times, cognitive technologies in their current form support or automate tasks, not entire jobs or processes. A key focus of this chapter, then, is to describe a number of tasks the technology can perform for businesses, and then to comment on how they can support business processes. For each technology I'll describe a set of typical process applications. Some of the tasks and applications are fully mature, and others will mature within the next several years—I'll try to make the maturity horizon clear in each case.

Similarly, cognitive technologies of today will have some impact on organizational structures and jobs. Since they generally augment humans rather than automating their jobs completely, they won't enable dramatic changes to organizational structures like running companies with few or no people. Their incremental effects, however, could make organizations of the near future feel substantially different than organizations do today. I'll describe likely organizational impacts of cognitive task capabilities for each technology capability as well.

In addition, it's important to remember that these technologies won't be implemented overnight. For each one there is a set of barriers and challenges to widespread and rapid implementation. So I'll include that topic in the discussion of each AI technology.

The remainder of this chapter, then, describes eight broad types of tasks that cognitive technologies can perform today. I've listed them in order of how widely they are currently used in businesses. No doubt this ranking will change; for example, moving autonomously around the world is ranked quite low, but as autonomous vehicle technology matures, its ranking will move up considerably. No doubt also they will all get better at the tasks over time—and I'll describe some of the likely improvement vectors and trajectories—but they're good enough now that organizational designers can begin to implement new structures and processes. Of course, one could cut these task categories differently; almost all of them involve, for example, finding patterns in data or creating models that fit structured or unstructured data. The emphasis here, however, is on describing tasks that organizations need to perform to meet their business missions.

Create Highly Granular Prediction and Classification Models

The task of creating and applying highly detailed statistical models is the forte of machine learning. It's like traditional statistical analysis on steroids; it can do several things that are virtually impossible with basic analytics. Those feats include learning from data to create highly effective models, producing many different models for a high level of granularity and fine tuning, and doing it all with relatively little effort from human analysts or data scientists. Instead of just machine learning, we might refer to this as "automated machine learning." If your organization has a lot of fast-changing numerical data and you want to make sense of it, this method is probably your best bet.

Machine learning is one of the broadest and most mature categories of AI technology, but we'll narrow it a bit for this discussion. I've already described the use of deep learning—a form of neural networks—for image and speech recognition. That is a form of machine learning, but for this discussion we'll focus only on machine learning that uses relatively traditional (and comprehensible) statistical models to predict or classify something. At the simplest end, it includes automated versions of basic regression analysis. More complex forms involve statistical algorithms like random forest, gradient boosting, decision trees, and the like. All of these are variations and combinations of basic statistical modeling approaches like regression analysis.

This type of machine learning, like basic analytics, is applicable to a very wide range of business phenomena with a lot of structured (i.e., numerical) data. It is perhaps most commonly used in marketing—particularly digital marketing, where it is the core of *programmatic buying*, or purchasing placement of digital ads on web publisher sites. It is used in sales to predict how likely a particular customer is to respond to a sales pitch—thus making much better use of a salesperson's time and energy. It's also heavily used in such areas as prevention of fraud and money laundering in banking, precision medicine (recommending treatments for patients based on detailed medical records and genomic information) in healthcare, approvals of claims in insurance, and intelligence and military applications in government. All of these applications have been used for more than a decade.

Machine learning can also be used to dramatically improve performance in application areas that have already been addressed with conventional analytics. Pricing optimization is a good example—also known as *revenue management*. It has been employed for several decades in airlines, hotels, and other industries, and was historically addressed using internal data (what products sold at what price) and econometric methods. But the combination of new external data sources and machine learning methods can yield dramatic improvements in profitability.

For example, the air charter firm XOJET, which has over 1,300 private jets available for charter, once used a simple set of spreadsheet rules derived from internal data to set prices. Now, however, with help from the machine learning technology company Noodle.ai, XOJET applies machine learning-based models to assess supply and demand and price their charter trips. They use external datasets that include industry-wide flight activity and aircraft location to establish competitive supply, and data on major demand-driving events, seasonal patterns, and booking curve observations to predict demand. Upon installing the new algorithm, the company's revenue per occupied flight rose 5 percent.

An additional XOJET application also assesses the popularity of destinations to assist in pricing decisions. Charter jets that fly to less popular destinations usually have to "deadhead" back with no passengers, which hurts both profitability and the environment. XOJET now uses a "fleet balance" machine learning application to predict demand for the day after a trip to/from a given origin/destination. As a result the company is flying fewer deadhead hours, which in turn boosts profitability. Other models predict the company's total fleet contribution for the day so far, and how that influences revenue and pricing targets over the next month.

Process Applications
As I noted above, these approaches can be used in a wide variety of business situations. Here are a few typical ones across multiple industries:

- Using external data to optimize pricing (as at XOJET)
- Pinpointing what digital ads are the best fit for a particular customer and publisher
- Creating detailed sales propensity models for customers and products
- Developing detailed precision medicine treatment recommendations
- Identifying potential fraud in banking and insurance
- Targeting anti–money laundering (AML) situations for human investigators

- Identifying customers who are likely to churn/attrit
- Predicting cybersecurity threats before they happen
- Deciding which people have the skills to staff a particular type of project
- Identifying insiders who might commit fraud or security violations
- Predicting energy assets that are worthy of further exploration

Organizational Implications

Overall, this type of AI is making possible more efficient, effective, and optimized business decisions. Some of the insights it generates will still be fed to a human decision maker—for example, a recommendation to a salesperson about which customer to call on next. Other decisions and actions will be taken directly by machines, as in what digital ad should be served up to you the next time you visit the *New York Times* website. Given the unreliability of human decision makers and the difficulty of interpreting machine learning, it's likely that more and more decisions will be made (and even executed) by machines over time. Some of those will be typical decisions made by middle managers, such as what person to assign to a particular project. Over time, that might reduce the role of middle management.[1]

Regardless of who makes the decision, however, there is typically too much data, and an answer is required too quickly, for the analysis to be done by traditional "artisanal" analytical methods. With this form of machine learning, a human analyst or data scientist is typically still required to kick off the analysis and turn AI programs loose on particular datasets, but far more models per quantitative expert can be accomplished with these tools. Either the organization will simply generate far more models with them, or somewhat fewer analytical people will be necessary over time to generate the same number of models.

These systems are already having a democratizing effect on data science. Because detailed knowledge of algorithms isn't always necessary to do this type of machine learning, the analysis can be done by people who aren't quantitative experts. One large bank, for example, found that a former ballerina with only an undergraduate degree in sociology could do some valuable machine learning analyses about which investments were most likely to rise if Donald Trump were elected president of the United States in 2016.

Some data scientists resist adoption of automated machine learning technology because they fear it will make them obsolete. My feeling, however, is that the only quantitative experts who will become obsolete are those that resist new technologies like these.

Challenges to Broad Implementation

Since this technology is relatively mature and is easier to use than many other AI technologies, technology itself is not a significant obstacle to broad implementation within organizations. Development skills, as noted above, are not as much an issue with this technology either as compared to other AI technologies like deep learning.

Data availability can be an obstacle, however. Machine learning works best when there is a lot of data available (thousands of cases or records, for example), and some of the data should be *labeled,* that is, where we know the outcome of the variable being predicted. If we were attempting, for example, to predict what factors might cause patients to get Type II diabetes, we'd need to know for a subset of patients (typically called the *training dataset*) whether they actually did contract the disease. This is called *supervised* machine learning, and it constitutes the great majority of machine learning in business. Many organizations find acquiring large amounts of labeled data problematic.

The other primary obstacle is—as with other AI tools—that many managers and other businesspeople don't know what's possible with machine learning. This problem is made somewhat more difficult by the wide range of tasks that are possible with the approach. Managers may need to be educated about the possibilities. One machine learning automation company, DataRobot (a company I advise), established "DataRobot University" to educate both users and executives about the value and use of machine learning.

At one large U.S. bank, for example, forty senior executives from a large business unit in the bank were educated about the technology—the vocabulary, typical applications, and ways that the technology is typically applied within financial services. The group spent an afternoon brainstorming ideas for applications within the bank. The last step in the education process was to identify six champions—managers responsible for frontline businesses—who would explore machine learning within their businesses. Now many production projects are underway using the machine learning models, including one to predict early loan repayment, and another to aggregate external data on privately held firms.

Perform Structured Digital Tasks

A relatively new but already mature technology, robotic process auto-mation (RPA), uses a combination of capabilities to perform structured, information-intensive digital tasks. RPA can't easily learn and needs to be taught what actions to take under what circumstances, but it can act autonomously and can accomplish useful functions in business. Owing in part to its simplicity and low cost, the returns on RPA projects are some of the highest of any AI-related technology. RPA implementa-tions (which often involve creation of visual process flow diagrams and some basic decision rules) can typically be done by nontechni-cal employees; some firms employ consultants, but some don't find a need for them. It's also the technology that is most likely to replace existing workers.

What constitutes a *structured digital task*? It's a repetitive activity that can be specified in advance with some precision, that involves rule-based decisions, and that involves accessing and inputting information from and to one or more information systems. The RPA system is inter-acting within a broader process as if it were a human user.

Processes or tasks that would not be well suited to RPA would include those requiring independent judgment, those for which all contingen-cies could not be predicted in advance, and those involving unpredict-able interactions with customers or employees. RPA does not generally include the ability to converse in natural language, although some implementations involve combinations of RPA and chatbots or intelli-gent agents.

Process Applications

- Identifying and reconciling records that don't match
- Replacing lost ATM or credit cards or other financial documents
- Transferring data from one system to another
- Comparing information in one system with that in another
- Automated generation of reports and textual content
- Reading and giving standard replies to emails and texts
- Accepting transactions or declaring exceptions
- Issuing receipts, confirmations, and other transactional notifications

Organizational Implications

The work now done by RPA systems was, of course, usually done by humans in the past. Since humans are not doing it anymore, we may infer either that those humans are no longer with the organization, or they are doing something else. Certainly there is some of the former, but not as much as you might think. Companies like the Swiss bank UBS are implementing thousands of RPA robots (really only instances of code running on servers) to do formerly human work, and their goal is to reduce employment. The company's CEO stated that the company is seeking cost savings through automation, and noted, "We make no secret that a certain portion of cost savings will come from reducing staff numbers."

UBS, like many large organizations, expects that a significant fraction of the cost savings will come from reducing or eliminating the need for outsourced workers. One might even say that if a job can be structured sufficiently to deploy it to an offshore outsourcer, it is likely to be doable with an RPA system—although of course there are exceptions. In reviewing a set of RPA projects in consulting engagements, substantially more outsourced jobs were already or planned to be reduced than jobs for employees.

But several organizations pursuing RPA implementation have found that RPA was more likely to lead to human workers doing something different than to them losing their jobs. It is common for organizations to have more work to do than their existing workforce can perform. At NASA, for example, RPA robots were not intended to replace workers at all, but to do "more work with the same workers." Human workers can of course address exceptions in processes identified by RPA, but can also monitor and improve the process in which RPA is performing key tasks. Or humans can explore and investigate situations that are too unstructured for an RPA robot to address.

Challenges to Broad Implementation

RPA is relatively inexpensive and easy to implement. So are there any obstacles that stand in the way of broad implementation? Yes, there are—but normally only when the number of robots implemented is quite substantial.

One problem is an IT architectural one. RPA robots become users of existing transaction or reporting systems. If the underlying system changes, the RPA system is likely to have to be reprogrammed. This is not a problem with a few robots, but if there are thousands of them the reprogramming effort would be quite substantial. Large numbers of robots also require organizations to keep accurate records of which robots perform what tasks and what systems they access in order to perform them.

A second challenge is more one of opportunity than problem. RPA implementation presents an opportunity to redesign the business process before automating it. Effective use of the technology could make processes faster, more efficient, and more reliable. Most firms are not sufficiently experienced in redesigning or reengineering business processes to take advantage of what RPA can accomplish.

For these reasons, firms that embark upon large-scale RPA implementation typically do so with a consultant. The consultant may help to undertake either the IT architecture or process redesign activities, or both. Without help, a company could find itself "wrapped in RPA spaghetti" or performing many process activities with robots that needn't be performed at all.

Manipulate Information

One of the least dramatic—but most valuable—cognitive capabilities is the ability to manipulate information to accomplish a business objective. Several variations on this capability exist. Perhaps the most common is to read text on paper, which is called optical character recognition (OCR). OCR has been around for decades, but it often required expert users to create templates for different types of characters and documents, and it was somewhat inflexible. Today AI-based OCR can read a wide variety of documents and characters without templates, and can read them not only from paper but also from various forms of electronic documents—emails, PDFs, and electronic forms.

After information has been extracted using OCR methods, it can be matched or combined in various ways. Big companies like GE, Thomson Reuters, and GlaxoSmithKline, for example, are using these tools to create one version of key information. They use *probabilistic matching* capabilities of machine learning (from a startup called Tamr, which I advise) to identify data across databases that is likely to be the same, even if it is slightly different. This was always possible with labor-intensive human methods, but now it is much faster. I've mentioned how GE was able to combine supplier data across the company. GlaxoSmithKline used the same approach to create unified repositories of clinical trials, assays (experiments), and genetic data—enabling scientists to analyze much larger and broader datasets than those from their own research.

A third way to manipulate data is to check it across multiple documents that are supposed to be the same, but may vary in practice. Another company I work with, RAGE Frameworks (now part of Genpact), does a lot of this work relative to contracts. It extracts the relevant data from contracts (e.g., the amount of product to be shipped by a supplier), and checks that against other relevant documents (e.g., the amount of product actually shipped in shipping notices or bills of lading). If the amounts don't match, someone can initiate a conversation with the supplier. A lot of imprecision exists in the world of business, and this type of document matching can squeeze some of it out.

Process Applications

Although somewhat prosaic, there are many applications of the ability of AI tools to manipulate information. A partial list includes:

• Automated extraction of multiple types of information from multiple types of documents and communications

- Ability to check contracts against delivered products and services
- Comparison of invoices to items actually shipped or received
- Ability to combine similar data records across multiple databases

Organizational Implications

Some workers do this type of work within companies, and might be subject to job loss if it is automated or partially automated. More common, however, are situations in which doing the tasks manually is so labor-intensive that organizations don't undertake them at all. In the unification of data area, for example, the large-scale performance of the task would require many data experts to address it and would take years. As a result, few organizations succeed at this objective.

The unification of data does open up possibilities for analysts and data scientists to analyze the data and find new meaning in it. This could lead to more job opportunities for these already-in-demand experts. It also opens up a wide range of possibilities for people to collaborate within organizations using common data.

Challenges to Broad Implementation

This application of AI for data manipulation is not terribly difficult in a technical sense, and the tools and human resources to do it are not that expensive. The greatest obstacle to broad implementation may be lack of awareness of the problems and the ability to solve them—perhaps because it is not a sexy or transformational objective. Managers may not realize, for example, that contracted services and products are frequently not actually delivered to them, or that invoices are often inaccurate. Consultants and vendors need to inform their customers that AI for data manipulation can yield far more value than it costs.

Understand Human Speech and Text

Understanding human language is one of the oldest goals of AI research and practice, but the technologies are getting much better at the task. We're now on the verge of being able to accomplish *conversational commerce*. As is also the case with image recognition, that improvement can be largely attributed to deep learning. Just as we turn an image into pixels and then an array of numbers whose pattern can be recognized by a statistical model, we can do the same with sound waves.

This application of AI is already pretty pervasive, and it is becoming more so. Chances are very good that your smartphone has it. Or you may have an inexpensive Amazon Echo or Google Home device. These machines all use deep learning to improve speech recognition, and they are all at roughly 95 percent accuracy. Andrew Ng, formerly of Stanford and Google and now the foremost AI researcher at China's Baidu, has helped propel that company's recognition accuracy even higher, to almost 99 percent. Ng argues that at 99 percent accuracy, speech will become the primary way we communicate with machines.[2]

Process Applications

If Ng is correct, that means there are a large number of current and future process applications of speech recognition technology. They include (as a partial list):

- Vehicle operations
- Online and mobile shopping
- Consumption of music and other forms of content
- Operation of industrial machinery
- Online testing and assessment in education
- Ordering of consumer and business products
- Online help and customer service/support

Of course, the success of these applications depends not only on the availability and accuracy of speech recognition, but also on the ability of organizations to structure information and knowledge well. In customer service/support applications, for example, an intelligent agent needs not only to understand what customers need (in the terms by which they ask for it), but also to be able to furnish correct answers. While some vendor advertisements might make one think that this is just a matter of "ingesting" documents with all the needed answers, it is rarely that simple a process.

And somewhat ironically, AI may diminish the long-term value of this AI-driven capability somewhat. As vehicles, industrial devices, and information systems become more intelligent and autonomous, there may be less of a need for humans to interact with them and tell them what to do. I don't see the need for speech with machines disappearing anytime soon, but there may be less of it in the future.

Organizational Implications

The primary tasks of many people in organizations involve interfacing with other humans using speech—in call or contact centers, for example. Some of them, of course, are likely to lose their jobs if machine-based speech recognition becomes broadly available. This is most likely to take away jobs that deal with highly structured information and customer interactions. Agents who deal with complex customer problems, or for whom emotional or empathetic capabilities are necessary in their jobs, are more likely to remain employed.

Companies could, of course, take employees who perform these structured interactions who are freed up by speech recognition and move them into roles like outbound customer contacts. At Danske Bank in Denmark, for example, the bank has identified (using machine learning of online behavior data) certain situations where customers were perceived to need advice—such as job changes with a new salary and pension plan. The bank then contacted these customers proactively and achieved 62 percent better results than in their traditional marketing campaigns. The outbound contact process is also used to reduce customer churn, which has also been effective. The bank has contacted over 20,000 customers and reduced churn by 70 percent.[3]

Some call centers exploring speech comprehension tools have also found that humans are better at machines in doing first-contact customer problem classification. Machines may not have the breadth of knowledge and terminology to be able to correctly identify the customer problem. Once the problem has been identified in terms that a computer system can understand, the logical next step may be to hand the customer off to a machine for detailed problem resolution.

Challenges to Broad Implementation

Three primary challenges to broad implementation can be identified. One is the possibility of poor service, or the perceptions of it by customers. Businesses have had automated speech recognition for many years (typically in the form of an *interactive voice response* or IVR system in a call center), and for many customers the quality has never been fully satisfactory. Many of us quickly hit the 0 key or yell "representative." It is possible, of course, that improved quality of speech recognition will overcome the poor service of the past, but it may take a while for consumer perceptions to become adjusted. Any shortcomings of speech recognition systems will confirm many users' doubts.

Beyond poor service, customer adoption of new behaviors may hinder or slow the adoption of speech recognition systems. Such systems, for example, are not widely used by drivers of cars even though they have been long available. Any new system will require the user to learn new skills and behaviors, and some will not be willing to make the investment.

Finally, as I suggested above, the knowledge graph behind a semantic (rather than statistical) speech recognition system may not be well-developed enough to foster widespread adoption of the technology. These systems will need to anticipate user questions and terminology, and provide the right type of assistance for a wide variety of customer needs. If the knowledge systems behind speech recognition don't work well, it won't be the fault of speech recognition, but the technology may be blamed anyway.

Plan and Optimize Operations

One of the primary activities that companies pursue with analytics and data is to plan and optimize operations; this has been a long-term focus of the *operations research* approach to analytics. It has always been done on a relatively small scale, however, using individual models with only a few variables. Cognitive tools—and machine learning in particular—can take this activity to the next level in breadth and depth.

AI may not be known for its role in manufacturing and operations, but there is an opportunity to use these tools to dramatically improve the efficiency and effectiveness of these important industries. Take, for example, the steel manufacturing startup Big River Steel, which is attempting a major transformation in this most industrial of industries.

Big River, based in Arkansas, makes extensive use of sensors, control systems, and machine learning-based optimization. Working with the AI consulting firm Noodle.ai, Big River has developed a variety of technologies to improve the practice and profit of steelmaking. Indeed, the company's CEO, David Stickler, often notes, "We are a technology company that happens to make steel."

Big River uses machine learning in six major areas, although each area varies in the maturity of the application:

• *Demand prediction*—Big River succeeds by using capital wisely, so it needs to accurately predict demand for steel. To do so it employs machine learning models using macroeconomic data, historical demand for steel, manufacturing activity, and the activity of large consumers of steel (e.g., housing starts, oil rig counts).

• *Sourcing and inventory management*—Like steel "minimills," Big River's raw material is scrap, so it needs to predict the availability of it. Noodle .ai has produced a "scrap index" and is working with Big River on a hedging approach for buying scrap steel.

• *Scheduling optimization*—What to produce when is an important decision for any steel mill, and it's particularly critical when one of your most important inputs is electrical energy (for arc furnaces that melt scrap into molten steel). The optimization models maximize energy consumption at off-peak times and thus minimize energy costs.

• *Production optimization*—All steel mills have unplanned events like breakouts (when molten steel breaks out of a mold during casting) and cobbles (when hot rolled steel escapes from rollers, often onto the mill floor). These events stop production and are both dangerous and costly. Machine learning models can predict when they are most likely to happen and minimize their occurrence.

• *Predictive maintenance*—As with an increasing number of industrial machines, Big River can use machine learning models to identify the optimal times to maintain key machines and equipment.

• *Outbound transportation optimization*—Companies like Amazon have long optimized their outbound supply chains, but this is much less common in steel mills. Big River works with customers and shippers to minimize the costs of outbound transportation and to optimize delivery windows for customers.

With each of these applications Big River and other firms have improved operations, but the most valuable benefits come from integrating them. Big River is attempting to create "end to end" optimization of the performance and profitability of the mill. The company already has models that interconnect different parts of business plans and operations and can optimize across the enterprise. This integrated approach to planning and optimization is still in its early stages, and refinement of it will require more data, tuning of algorithms, and substantial computing horsepower. But both Stickler and the data scientists at Noodle .ai are convinced that it is possible.

Process Applications

The examples of applications at Big River Steel are suggestive of the planning and optimization applications possible through cognitive technologies. Some others include:

• Supply chain forecasting and stockout prediction
• Demand planning and forecasting for particular products or categories
• Reinforcement learning based on past decision data
• Evaluating the impact of sales promotions and incentives
• Predicting and minimizing unplanned production outages
• Modeling supply chain networks and operations with real-time updating
• Planning optimal shipping routes based on traffic and weather

Organizational Implications

This type of application could lead to fewer workers in factories, as more decisions and tasks are automated. But it also means that those who have jobs will require higher levels of skills and knowledge, will be paid more, and will probably be in less dangerous jobs. At Big River

Steel, for example, operators have to understand data and interpret dashboards—usually in control rooms rather than on the mill floor. They are compensated in part based on hitting production and profit targets, and as a result their average pay is far higher than at other U.S. steel mills.

Very few people have been trained for this type of large-scale AI-driven operations, since it didn't exist in the past. That means that there will be a large need for retraining of the work force. It also means high demand for experienced AI hands who can develop such models—either within companies or at consulting/technology firms.

Perceive and Recognize Images

A key AI task that has seen considerable advancement over the last decade is the ability to perceive and recognize images—sometimes known as *computer vision* or *machine vision*. It existed for more than two decades, but it wasn't very accurate. Image recognition by machines is now at the level of human vision in many domains, and better in some cases. These technologies are not widely used in business yet (outside of online firms like Google and Facebook), but they have the potential to be.

The underlying technology behind contemporary image recognition is deep learning neural networks; the other facilitating development is the availability of large numbers of labeled images. Most applications of machine vision do supervised learning and require a large number of labeled images from which to learn. In other words, the only reason that Google was able to develop a model to identify cat pictures on the internet is a complex deep learning algorithm, which was trained on many cat photos that are clearly identified as "cat."

But image recognition in business is beginning to move beyond simple examples like recognizing cats on the internet. A startup named Doxel, for example, is using deep learning image recognition to scan 3D images (taken by robots) of construction sites.[4] It classifies images of subprojects in terms of how close to being finished they are. The objective is to determine whether the overall project is likely to meet estimates or guarantees of timely completion. In an industry where late and over-budget projects are often the norm, a system like this could be very helpful to project managers if it works.

Process Applications

Image recognition has a wide variety of applications. A very partial list (most of which are available in some form today) includes:

- Monitoring of construction projects for completion times
- Recognition of road signs and markings, other cars, and pedestrians in autonomous vehicles
- Recognition of what customers buy in retail (e.g., Amazon Go convenience stores)
- Recognition of product defects in manufacturing production lines
- Facial recognition in retail and technology (e.g., Apple iPhone X)
- Identification and classification of apparel
- Identification of problematic aspects of medical images
- Classifying or describing online photos (e.g., in Facebook or Google Photos)

Organizational Implications

Some image recognition applications have major implications for organizations—mostly in terms of possible job losses, or at least major changes in how people do their work. Autonomous vehicles powered by this technology, for example, have the potential to eliminate many driving jobs—in taxis, trucks, ships, delivery vehicles, and so forth—although they have not done so yet. Image recognition and analysis for medical images have the potential to replace human radiologists, although this has not yet happened.

Recognition of what customers buy in stores could replace human point-of-sale cashiers. As Amazon describes the process at its pilot Go stores:

Our checkout-free shopping experience is made possible by the same types of technologies used in self-driving cars: computer vision, sensor fusion, and deep learning. Our Just Walk Out Technology automatically detects when products are taken from or returned to the shelves and keeps track of them in a virtual cart. When you're done shopping, you can just leave the store. Shortly after, we'll charge your Amazon account and send you a receipt.[5]

There has been speculation about how few humans might be needed to staff stores like Amazon Go, but no details from Amazon. My own visits to the store in Seattle suggested that humans are there to help customers enter the store with the Go app, to check IDs when buying alcoholic beverages, and to clean up spills. Zeynep Ton, who researches how retailers and other employers provide good jobs to employees, notes that machines are unlikely to do everything in such stores:

Even if self-checkout prevails, most of the work at retail stores will still be done by employees. Customers will not be invited to receive merchandise on the loading dock, shelve merchandise, move merchandise between storage locations and the selling floor, or change prices.[6]

Image recognition of photos on the internet has thus far not had major impact on jobs and organizations either. Companies like Facebook and YouTube certainly have algorithms designed to detect pornographic or terrorist images, but they generally work by flagging potentially problematic photos for human content checkers to evaluate further. Despite this two-level process, the company still occasionally makes mistakes.[7] And it is likely, of course, that without the AI algorithms, substantially more people would be needed to review content. However, these types of jobs are relatively new, and their numbers still seem to be growing rather than shrinking. YouTube has announced, for example, that it will increase its "content moderation" workforce to over 10,000 people in 2018.[8]

In general, the failure of the technology to create major impacts on organizations is primarily due to two factors. One, the technology is not entirely mature yet. Visual perception and recognition through deep learning promises to be as good as or better than humans at some point, but it's not entirely there yet, and there isn't enough labeled data to learn from.

Two, making major change in organizational arrangements and jobs would require substantial organizational and process change for established organizations. Amazon was smart to try out these new processes in an entirely new organization—Amazon Go—but it will surely find them more difficult to implement in the Whole Foods chain that it acquired.

Challenges to Broad Implementation

Any organization will face several challenges to broad implementation of image recognition as it rolls out the technology. Difficult boundary conditions are one key barrier. In autonomous vehicles, for example, identifying pedestrians, other vehicles, roads, lane markers, and road signs during a snowstorm would be challenging for any current technology.

Problematic boundary conditions also are found in retail applications of image recognition. According to one account, Amazon Go faced a couple of these early on:

Amazon has run into problems tracking more than about 20 people in the store at one time, as well as the difficulty of keeping tabs on an item if it has been moved from its specific spot on the shelf.[9]

It is certainly possible that boundary conditions will ease over time as deep learning technology improves. However, it is important for organizations adopting this technology for image recognition to understand the limitations at the time they implement it.

Privacy and "creepiness" issues can also inhibit image recognition. The most common application for concern in this regard is with facial recognition. Privacy issues arise with regard to retail environments; intelligence, crime, and other government applications; and even personal technology. It is technically possible for store chains to employ facial recognition today to recognize frequent customers, but concerns about privacy and the "creepiness factor" have prevented it. In government, the greatest concern is, as the American Civil Liberties Union puts it:

The biggest danger is that this technology will be used for general, suspicionless surveillance systems. State motor vehicles agencies possess high-quality photographs of most citizens that are a natural source for face recognition programs and could easily be combined with public surveillance or other cameras in the construction of a comprehensive system of identification and tracking.[10]

Current technology is already capable of recognizing faces in a crowd, which raises concerns about governmental monitoring of protests or civil disobedience.

Finally, there is the challenge that deep learning systems require—in most commercial applications anyway—labeled images for the models to learn from. Labeling images is labor-intensive and must generally be done by humans. Some open source databases like ImageNet have already incorporated previous labeling work by humans, but they contain only certain classes of images (many cats, for example). If your organization plans to use supervised deep learning for some proprietary visual asset (say, your apparel line), you'll have to figure out how to label many images.

Move Purposefully and Autonomously Around the World

The combination of new forms of AI, new or less expensive sensors, and traditional robotics means that smart machines are increasingly able to navigate the world and accomplish mobile tasks without human intervention. Autonomous vehicles are the most obvious example of this phenomenon, but robots moving around factories and warehouses are another. In a highly mobile world the ability to move people and things around without human drivers is a dramatic change, which is why this category has attracted so much attention.

The concept of autonomous vehicles is well understood, but the exact level of autonomy they will achieve by what time is still uncertain. Level 3 autonomy, for example, which is already available from several car manufacturers, means that vehicles can operate autonomously under many circumstances, but a human driver is still required to be available to take over. Level 4 vehicles are fully autonomous, but only under certain circumstances—slow speeds or certain road types, for example. Level 5 autonomy implies a fully autonomous vehicle under all circumstances. While the greatest benefits for both businesses and consumers accrue from full autonomy, there are some benefits from partial autonomy as well—for example, a truck that can drive autonomously on highways while a driver sleeps, with the driver taking over in cities.

In addition to autonomous vehicles, robots are making strides (so to speak) in this category. Companies are already using robots to prepare food, assist shoppers, deliver room service meals, and engage banking customers at the door. They can move not only around offices, factories, or warehouse floors (common, for example, in Amazon's distribution centers), but also outside, across uneven terrain in unfamiliar environments. Boston Dynamics robots, for example, travel across terrain on two legs, four legs, or a combination of wheels and legs, depending on the model. They can even pick themselves up after falling, which earlier robots were unable to do.

Robots are also becoming more collaborative. In factories they used to be cordoned off from humans because any contact between humans and machines was dangerous (for the humans). A new generation of light-duty robots, however, can work alongside human workers, and can be easily trained by nonexpert workers.

Other changes in robotics that have contributed to their fast pace of improvement in the past several years are the rise of open-source robot operating systems, the proliferation of low-cost sensors, and the convergence of robot perceptual and logical capabilities with broader, more powerful AI systems from other contexts.[11] An IDC report predicts that spending on robots will hit \$135 billion by 2019.[12]

Process Applications

Of course, many potential process applications of these technologies exist for both businesses and consumers. Some are available today, while others are just around the corner. Here's a partial list:

- Autonomous delivery of goods for businesses (probably more than a decade away)
- Autonomous driving of humans in taxis and ride services (perhaps in five years or less within controlled areas of cities
- Autonomous driving of humans in private vehicles (five to ten years?)
- Autonomous flight by drones and eventually airplanes/helicopters (five years for drones, more than a decade for aircraft with human passengers)
- Multiple manufacturing applications (already being used)
- Warfighting applications (used today for identifying and exploding IEDs)

• Movement of high weight or volume goods around factories and warehouses (widely used today by companies like Amazon)
• Care of elderly or bedridden patients (piloted in Japan today on a small scale)
• Cleaning houses or performing other domestic tasks (already done in part by technologies like iRobot)
• Autonomous farming (already used, for example, for thinning lettuce crops from a startup, Blue River, acquired by John Deere[13])
• Care of domestic and farm animals (robotic milking of cows is widely used)

Organizational Implications

The role of human drivers in a world of autonomous vehicles is one of the most discussed issues in AI. The American Trucking Association estimates that there are about 3.5 million truck drivers in the United States, and some fraction of them may well at some point be out of work. The same might be said for the roughly 200,000 taxi drivers in the United States, and the approximately half a million ride-sharing drivers.

Of course, even when fully autonomous driving becomes available, not all of these drivers will lose their jobs. Not all owners of trucks, taxis, and ride-sharing vehicles will upgrade quickly. Some former behind-the-wheel drivers will monitor vehicles remotely; others will provide driving services to customers who need extra help, or "white glove" delivery services. It is very likely, however, that we will need fewer people in these roles at some point—almost certainly within a decade.

Even with partial autonomy, somewhat fewer drivers may be necessary. Perhaps partially autonomous trucks will be able to drive longer distances with a single driver, and perhaps drivers will not be necessary in all ride-sharing services. These job reductions are likely enough so that families, companies, and governments should begin planning for a post-driving future.

Within factories and warehouses, job losses from robots have been taking place for a while. Research by two economists of the impact of robots on local labor markets concludes that, between 1990 and 2007, adding one industrial robot per thousand workers reduced employment in America by about six workers.[14] And as I have noted, the robots during this period were less qualified than those available today, and perhaps less likely to fully replace human workers.

However, robots don't always displace workers. Amazon, for example, has deployed over 100,000 robots in its distribution centers and warehouses, many of which are from Kiva Systems—a company it acquired in 2012. But since beginning to deploy those robots in 2014, Amazon has added over 80,000 jobs in warehouses.[15] Of course, it helps that Amazon's volume of business has increased dramatically over that period.

I'll discuss this issue in greater detail in chapter 6. For now, we'll have to leave it that smart machines that move—autonomous vehicles and robots—are a considerable threat to human employment. But it's not at all clear how quickly this threat will materialize, and how many jobs will ultimately be lost as a result.

The advent of many autonomous vehicles will also have impacts on the structure and functions of cities and of supply chains. We don't know yet what it will mean for commuting, for optimal office locations, and for re-architected supply networks, but it's not too early for companies to start thinking about those issues. Real estate decisions have long lead times and can play out over decades.

Challenges to Broad Adoption

The challenges to broad adoption of smart machines that move are similar to those for technologies that "perceive and recognize images," since image recognition is also critical in this context. I discussed these as "boundary conditions" earlier in this chapter. The same issues involved in "identifying pedestrians, other vehicles, roads, lane markers, and road signs during a snowstorm" apply here as well.

Installed base issues are another constraint to broad adoption. Neither consumers nor companies will adopt the most sophisticated technologies immediately. That means that many older, nonautonomous vehicles will be on the road for a long time. In addition, the combination of autonomous and nonautonomous vehicles could make for difficult driving. For example, MIT robotics researcher John Leonard is fond of showing a video in which he tries to turn left into a long line of bumper-to-bumper traffic. He argues that it will be even more difficult for autonomous vehicles to persuade human drivers to allow the merge. Interactions between autonomous vehicles and human pedestrians are also likely to be quite challenging.[16] One pedestrian has already been killed by an autonomous Uber vehicle (with an inattentive human driver as a backup) in Arizona in 2018.

There may also be regulatory or public reaction issues in adoption of autonomous vehicles. Thus far, regulatory agencies have been largely open to the testing of autonomous vehicles. At least forty-seven cities around the world have approved autonomous vehicle pilots. But this could change if the public reacts negatively to accidents, or unfairly blames autonomous vehicles over human drivers for them. Data suggest that while a majority of survey respondents would like to own an autonomous vehicle, a majority does not consider them safe.[17]

Assess Human Emotions

One set of tasks that is not commonly associated with AI is the assessment of human emotions. This development is still in its early stages, but several startups have products on the market that purport to assess emotions. The primary method employed is machine learning analysis of facial expressions from images or video. Based on this analysis, companies claim to be able to detect "micro-expressions" that may not be identified by human eyes, and some even argue that they can use these expressions to understand underlying personality traits and behavioral tendencies. Most of these companies are relatively recent spinouts of university research labs.

The most common usage of this capability is in sales and marketing. Companies that want to understand how customers feel about their products or services can analyze their facial expressions to find out. Affectiva, for example, an MIT Media Lab spinout (from the Affective Computing research group), uses both facial and vocal expressions to assess whether customers like products, advertisements, media content, and so forth. The company says its algorithms learn from over five million facial videos and two billion facial images within them. The company often works with consumer goods companies and uses market researchers or advertising agencies as intermediaries.

There are other applications beyond sales and marketing, however, as well as technologies for emotion assessment beyond facial analysis. Facebook, for example, has attempted to make progress toward the goal of predicting suicide among the site's users before they happen. The primary technology employed is AI-based analysis of speech in videos and text. Potentially problematic content is then reviewed (quickly, one hopes) by human Facebook employees. The initiative is partly in response to a series of live-streamed suicides on the site in 2017. Some have argued, however, that it is very difficult for even trained clinicians to predict suicide attempts, and that AI-based analyses would inevitably be less sophisticated.[18]

A move is also underway to create "social robots" that would serve as effective companions for humans—for example, the otherwise-isolated elderly. A necessary component of this companion role is clearly the ability to assess emotion in humans. The earliest social robots available today (for example, Jibo—another MIT spinout from the Affective Computing area of the Media Lab), however, don't have the ability to assess emotion.

Process Applications

It is early days for the use of emotion assessment in business, but here are some current and potential applications:[19]

• Assessing on a large scale what customers think of various types of online content—for example, ads, and online media (social media sentiment analysis is widely employed today)

• Virtual market research for potential new products and services (done today on a small scale)

• Evaluation of driver moods (e.g., "road rage") and potential safety in autonomous vehicles (done on a small scale today, with questionable accuracy)

• High-level diagnosis of various personality traits and problems (only in research labs today)

• Identifying perplexity or boredom in online education (technically possible but not yet available)
• Making "social robot" companions more empathetic (they exist in primitive form today)
• Reacting to moods and emotions in online gaming (possible today, but not widely used)
• Understanding the impact of emotion on health status and health interventions (only in labs)
• Assessment of the emotional state of animals (e.g., detecting pain levels in sheep[20]—only in research labs)

Organizational Implications

The large-scale (but relatively shallow) analysis of human emotion is not an activity that most organizations currently pursue. Therefore, it is relatively unlikely that the application will have major negative implications for employees of businesses. Indeed, the rise of automated emotion assessment may give rise to new jobs. Facebook announced in 2017 that it planned to add 3,000 more workers to its 4,500-employee "community operations" function.[21] This group reviews posts and other content reported for violent, suicidal, or otherwise troubling content. Since the automated assessment of emotion is often not sufficiently reliable on its own to be the basis for action, detection of potential problems usually results in further investigation by humans.

If this technology matures further, it could have implications for the large number of human workers who deal with human psyches. Psychiatrists, clinical psychologists, social workers, and other mental health clinicians could have their jobs augmented—or perhaps even replaced to some degree—by these technologies. However, this seems a long way off, and it may never be possible, for reasons that are detailed in the section below.

Challenges to Broad Implementation

This area of automated emotion analysis relies on signals that are difficult and ambiguous to interpret. Whether the data source is human facial expression or human words in speech and text, accurately translating those signals into valid human emotions is difficult for trained experts, and is even more difficult for machines. In the case of human facial expressions, challenges exist even in identifying faces in videos and images, not to mention the difficulties of extracting relevant facial features and determining how they represent emotions.[22] Human linguists have difficulty even classifying whether social media comments are positive, negative, or neutral—and have much less success in determining how they translate into true emotions of their creators.

Given these difficulties, I believe that automated assessment will continue to be a "first pass" analysis at human emotions, and that detailed analysis by humans will be necessary in circumstances requiring in-depth understanding of emotions. In other words, automated assessment won't replace psychiatry or clinical psychology, but it may be able to provide a quick, semiaccurate reading of how online content appeals to humans, or how captured images and videos reveal certain emotional attributes of their subjects.

The Need for Process Architecture or (Re)Engineering

In the early 1990s, one of the most important management trends (I know because I wrote the first article and book on it) was business process reengineering (BPR).[23] This set of ideas, which encouraged order-of-magnitude improvement in broad business processes, was advanced in best-selling books and led to considerable activity among consulting firms. The primary drivers of the BPR movement were a need for substantially improved productivity (in part because of a perceived threat from Japanese competitors) and a powerful new set of information technologies. These technologies included enterprise resource planning (ERP) systems, direct connections between customers and suppliers, and the then-nascent Internet.

Some of the same opportunities and threats are present today. Productivity growth in the United States, Western Europe, and Japan has languished for several years, and some prominent economists have proclaimed that information technologies have never fueled the productivity improvements of which they might be capable.[24] The primary threat perceived by many established firms is no longer large Japanese competitors, but rather nimble startups in regions like Silicon Valley.

Cognitive technologies are the current equivalent of disruptive technologies for processes. As in the 1990s, this generation of AI can become a driver of work transformation. Also as in the 1990s, the desired transformation won't take place through technology alone.

It may be time, then, for the rebirth of BPR—this time with a specific focus on AI as an enabler of process change. The marriage seems a good match. Cognitive technologies need a set of management structures and best implementation practices to yield the benefits of which they are capable. And BPR, which was perhaps overly ambitious in the first place, and which went astray in the 1990s as a label for large-scale job cuts[25], could use some rehabilitation of its image.

Companies are just beginning to seize on the work redesign idea from AI. Thus far, many have "paved the cow path" by automating the existing work process. This is particularly the case with robotic process automation technology. As I suggested in chapter 3, simply automating existing workflows can be a fast way to get to implementation and ROI, but it misses an opportunity for substantial improvement in the process.

BPR can also be viewed as an instance of *design thinking*, a set of loosely structured techniques for envisioning new products or ways of doing business. According to Tim Brown, the CEO of IDEO (where the approach was pioneered):

Design thinking is a human-centered approach to innovation that draws from the designer's toolkit to integrate the needs of people, the possibilities of technology, and the requirements for business success.

Design thinking has largely been developed since the first generation of reengineering, and it is a broader and less structured approach. At least one cognitive technology expert—Manoj Saxena, the chairman of AI startup Cognitive Scale, and the former IBM Watson general manager, argued that design thinking was a useful method for harnessing cognitive technology.[26]

It will probably also be useful to employ some of the typical tools used in BPR and other process-centric methods, such as understanding and measuring the current process, and laying out the steps and flows of the "to be" process. In addition, it's key to describe the specific "division of labor" between humans and machines at different steps within the process. One call center company, for example, determined that only humans were able to deal with the breadth of call topics from customers calling in for service. So they employ humans for initial triage of calls, and then connect customers to one of more than a thousand "bots" to handle detailed questions. Another company—a financial asset management and brokerage firm—chose the opposite approach, designing the bot to handle first line questions, and humans to address detailed questions on particular topics. There's no right answer to this sort of question—only one that fits your situation and strategy.

The keys to cognitive-driven BPR are to explicitly focus on processes, to strive for ambitious levels of change, and to pay considerable attention to organizational change management issues. It's also important to involve those who do the work today in the redesign process, so sending out messages that "augmentation" will be the order of the day rather than "automation" will facilitate their involvement.

6 Jobs and Skills in a World of Smart Machines

Most of the predictions and accounts of the job impacts of AI have focused on the bad news. Millions of jobs can be automated, these accounts suggest. Those at the lower end of the socioeconomic spectrum have the most to fear. Evil bosses will substitute machines for labor without a second thought. Unless a minimum basic income is established, inequality will grow until there are riots in the streets. Even if some new jobs are created, there won't be enough to avoid social and economic dislocation.

These concerns could turn out to be true. As you've already read in this book, cognitive technologies will be able to perform many tasks with a high degree of autonomy. They are likely to create substantial upheaval in job markets. New skills will inevitably be required. But after researching this topic for several years, I am convinced that there will not be massive job loss from automation anytime soon.

Of course, nobody knows for sure what's going to happen in the future of work (or any other future, for that matter). There are four things that we can do to try to get a sense of what will happen with jobs and skills because of AI, however. One is to extrapolate from the past and the present, although many people believe that cognitive technologies will get a lot smarter quickly—making extrapolation less reliable. Two, we can look at the details of contemporary jobs and tasks and assess how many of them can be automated in the near future. Three, we can employ surveys and ask practicing managers what they think is going to happen with jobs. And four, we can employ logic to debate how likely automation will be. I'll use each of those approaches in this chapter—we need all the tools we can get!

In the next couple of sections I'll review both the case for large-scale automation and the (more likely) case for marginal automation and broad "augmentation" of human workers by AI and vice-versa. Managers generally find the idea of automation appealing from both cost reduction and operational performance perspectives. On the other hand, augmentation tends to provide more flexibility and potential for innovation, and large-scale automation is often difficult to accomplish. I'll then describe how companies can move forward on either their automation or augmentation strategies, although I believe augmentation is both a more likely and more desirable future.

The Case for Large-Scale Automation

Let's face it—artificial intelligence is a powerful tool, and it can do—more or less by itself after being programmed—a broad range of things. My conclusion after the IBM Watson *Jeopardy!* win (against the best human players) and the Alphabet Go win (against one of the best human players) was that if we set our minds to teaching a task—any task—to cognitive systems we will ultimately be successful. And "successful" means the ability to do that task better than a human.

The concern about large-scale automation probably reached its peak in 2015, when books like Martin Ford's *Rise of the Robots*[1] and Jerry Kaplan's *Humans Need Not Apply*[2] acquainted readers with the idea that AI was improving rapidly, humans were not, and technology was likely to replace many workers across a variety of industries and business functions.

This logic and some further investigation informed a series of predictions about how likely AI is to take over human jobs. The method employed in these predictions is usually to break down jobs into their constituent tasks, and then assess how likely future AI (often at an unspecified future date) will be able to perform that task. If a majority or sizable minority of the tasks can be performed by a smart machine, the job is classified as "automatable."

The earliest of this type of prediction came in 2013 from Karl Benedikt-Frey and Michael Osborne, two researchers at Oxford University. They analyzed the percentage of jobs that could be automated based on the tasks they performed. For jobs in the United States, they determined that 47 percent were likely to be automated by 2033 based on task analysis and low levels of "bottlenecks to computerization."[3] The same Oxford authors, working on another study using similar methods, concluded that 35 percent of U.K. jobs could be automated over the next ten to twenty years.[4] These studies, perhaps offering a higher level of precision than is warranted about the future, received a high degree of attention in the press.

Several other researchers in universities and consulting firms have used similar methods. An OECD-sponsored paper by several researchers from Germany argued that Frey and Osborne's study focused on the automatability of entire jobs rather than tasks (the jobs were broken down into tasks in the Oxford study, but the entire job was rated for automation potential). Given that jobs typically consist of a series of tasks, they argued that the number of nonautomatable tasks in many jobs meant that the overall level of job automation would be much lower—9 percent on average across 21 OECD countries.[5]

A PWC study attempted to reconcile the diverse findings of these two studies—that is, 47 percent vs. 9 percent—and concluded that the OECD study overcorrected for the task vs. jobs issue. These researchers argued that the best prediction was 38 percent in the United States and 30 percent in the United Kingdom. They raised the important caveat that "not all of these technologically feasible job automations may occur in practice for the economic, legal and regulatory reasons" they elaborate in their paper.[6] However, they did not estimate the impact of these other factors on job loss percentages.

In 2015 McKinsey Global Institute researchers used job breakdowns into tasks to predict that 45 percent of jobs (representing $2 trillion in compensation for U.S. workers) could be automated using current, but leading edge, technologies. They predicted that an additional 13 percent of jobs could be automated with better natural language processing technologies.[7]

In a 2017 report, however, the McKinsey researchers made an important addition to their methodology. They pointed out that whether a job was technically automatable was only one of several factors determining whether it would be automated over a certain timeframe. Four other factors they identified include:

- costs to automate
- the relative scarcity, skills, and cost of workers who might otherwise do the activity
- benefits (e.g., superior performance) of automation beyond labor-cost substitution
- regulatory and social-acceptance considerations

While 45 percent of jobs might be technically automatable, the McKinsey researchers stated that fewer than 5 percent of 830 U.S. occupations are candidates for "full automation" given existing technology capabilities and these other influences.[8]

The automation-of-jobs literature, then, suggests that between 5 percent and 47 percent of jobs will be automated over the next couple of decades. No one knows the right answer, but for the reasons I describe below, I'd argue that the number will be much closer to 5 percent than 47 percent.

One reason for my lower-bound estimate is that automation is hard. The technology has to be really good to fully entrust a set of tasks to it. The tasks that the machines can accomplish have to be broad enough to replace entire jobs. The organization has to figure out a new work process and what to do with the people who previously performed it. There may be some legal or regulatory challenges to full automation. It's no wonder that I and at least some other observers expect that the amount of it will be relatively small.

Certainly some managers desire automation because they feel it will make their companies more cost-competitive, or their customers more satisfied. Assuming that the automation doesn't happen on an economy-wide scale and that there will still be customers with jobs who can afford to buy their offerings, automation could be good for the companies and the overall economy.

The Case for Large-Scale Augmentation

As I suggested above, I believe *augmentation*—smart humans working in collaboration with smart machines—is by far more likely than
large-scale automation. There are a number of reasons for this, and I'll
describe five of them below. If you want more detail on this topic, Julia
Kirby and I wrote a book on it in 2016.[9] We argued that augmentation also has strategic benefits, in that it is more conducive to rapid
and frequent innovation in business processes and models. We strongly
emphasized the likelihood of augmentation, and we haven't changed
our minds since then.

First, as some of the automation research cited suggests, *AI tends to
support or automate tasks, not entire jobs.* Almost every job consists of a
variety of tasks. While the mix of automatable vs. nonautomatable tasks
varies across job types, relatively few jobs have so many structured and
quantitative tasks that they can be fully automated. At some point, perhaps, cognitive technologies will be able to do everything that humans
can do, only better. At this point of "singularity," of course, all bets
about potential job loss are off. It's also worth mentioning that some of
the tasks that smart machines can automate are likely to be managerial
ones, not just those performed by lower-level employees.

A second reason augmentation is more likely is that surveys suggest
that *most managers neither want nor expect large-scale automation.* In a
Deloitte 2017 survey of "cognitive aware" managers, for example, only
6 percent of respondents ranked "reduce headcount through automation" as their primary objective for using cognitive technologies—the
lowest among nine alternatives—and only 22 percent put in in their
top three priorities—again the lowest among all options.

In the same survey, the percentage of respondents expecting substantial job loss from AI-driven automation varied from 11 percent in
three years, to 14 percent in five years, and 22 percent in ten years
(see figure 6.1). Except for the ten-year prediction, these numbers were
substantially lower than the percentages expecting more optimistic
outcomes—new jobs from AI, augmentation of workers by AI and
vice-versa, or no real change in jobs. Even in ten years, 28 percent of

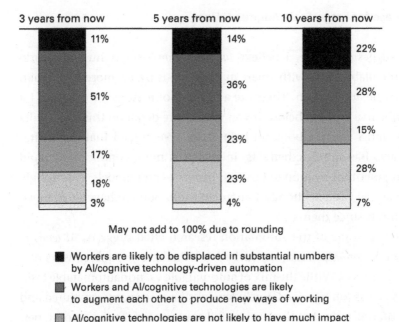

Figure 6.1
Predictions about Job Futures over Different Timeframes
Source: 2017 Deloitte "Cognitive Aware" Survey

managers in the survey expected "many new jobs" from AI/cognitive technology, versus the 22 percent expecting substantial job loss.

Other surveys find similar results. In a 2017 McKinsey survey, for example, the companies that have most aggressively adopted AI are pursuing growth from the technology rather than cost savings.[10] In a Genpact-sponsored survey by Fortune Knowledge Group, AI leaders are very likely (96 percent agreement) to believe that AI will transform their workforce, but substantial majorities expect that humans will move to more complex work and that there will be a need for reskilling employees.[11] In another Cognizant survey of 5,000 consumers in three English-speaking countries, only 10 percent strongly agree that AI threatens their jobs today.[12]

In a survey I participated in of 152 consulting projects using automation technologies, virtually none involved substantial employee

job loss thus far. The jobs lost primarily involved outsourced workers, and no projects involved more than 100 lost jobs of any type.
Some projects did have plans to eliminate jobs, but the numbers in the
plans were still quite small. Many planned to keep the same number
of workers and be able to grow using cognitive technologies without
adding employees.[13]

A third factor in the argument that massive automation will not take
place is *experience from previous generations of technology*. Boston University economist James Bessen, for example, has pointed out that there
are still about the same number of bank tellers in the United States as
there were in 1980, despite technologies such as ATMs and internet
home banking that would seem to threaten this occupation.[14]

A study by Dana Remus and Frank Levy on the impact of automation
technologies on the legal profession finds that while lawyers' jobs have
been substantially changed by technology, there has been little if any
job loss.[15] In a blog post, radiologist Luke Oakden-Rayner argues that
for radiologists to lose their jobs from automation, more than 5 percent
of radiology images would have to be fully automated each year—and
that this is unlikely to happen given current technology trends and
capabilities.[16]

A fourth reason automation is less likely than augmentation is that
people find new jobs and tasks to perform when previous tasks are taken
over by automation. Insurance underwriters, for example, haven't dis-
appeared even though rule-based underwriting has automated much of
their traditional roles of approving and pricing insurance policies. Some
have moved into jobs involving communicating with customers and
insurance agents about policy applications and approvals. Others monitor the automated systems themselves, and some monitor the outcomes
of automated underwriting decisions in terms of an insurance company's
broad risk portfolio. Some have lost their jobs, and insurance underwriting is not considered a growth profession.

In my research on the implications of AI, I have observed many
examples of jobs—from elementary school teachers, to lawyers, to
dermatologists—in which some aspect of the job had been automated,
but new roles and skills emerged to give people plenty to do. For example, in a "School of One" in New York where decisions about what

content to provide to students had been taken over by an adaptive learning system, a teacher I interviewed spends a lot of time interpreting what the system is recommending for students, recommending new learning strategies and behaviors, and exploring new software and content sources. Although educational content is increasingly online and adaptive learning systems do an excellent job of serving the right content to students, no one is proposing that teachers are no longer necessary.

A fifth and final reason massive job loss is not a concern is that *a lot of entirely new jobs will be created*. Digital marketers, for example, hold jobs that probably wouldn't exist without the automation in that field. It simply wouldn't be feasible, for example, to go through a quick price auction and place personalized and targeted digital ads on publishers' sites in milliseconds without so-called programmatic buying based on machine learning. But there is still a variety of tasks for which human digital marketers are necessary, and they are able to be substantially more productive than the marketers of old because of the automation.

Others have addressed the issue of new jobs as well. Gartner Inc., the market research firm, predicted (without any discussion of its prediction methods) that while there would be a substantial number of jobs lost to AI in the short run, within three years from 2017 the increase in net jobs would be positive as a result of new AI-related jobs. By 2025, the firm argues, there will be two million net new jobs.[17]

The consulting firm Cognizant's Center for the Future of Work has identified twenty-one jobs that will be created over the next ten years, most of which depend on AI in some way.[18] There's the AI-Assisted Healthcare Technician and the Man-Machine Teaming Manager, for example. It is of course impossible to know for sure whether such jobs (and such titles) will materialize, but very likely that some new jobs will emerge—some of which even consultants can't dream up.

One of the most cogent arguments for new jobs in the Cognizant report is this one:

Technology solves—and creates—problems. The guilty little secret of the technology world is that every solution begets a problem. Fix A, and then B goes on the fritz. Develop C—which is a great new thing—and then realize you've also created D—which is a terrible new thing that needs fixing. Intelligent machines will address many problems in society (see above), but in doing so, they will also create lots of new problems that people will need to work on addressing. Work that they will monetize. The work ahead goes on forever.

This is similar to the argument made by Jeanne Ross of MIT in a recent short article. She argues that "the outputs of most automated processes require people to do something."[19] I have seen this issue arise in a variety of enterprise situations. Several companies in the financial services industry, for example, use a system from the company Digital Reasoning (disclosure: the company once sent me a cool T-shirt and jacket) to monitor employee communications for potential fraud or malfeasance. The company's technology is good enough to suggest a high potential for investigation, but not quite good enough to accuse and fire the likely offender—so that final step (after some more investigation) has to be taken by humans.

The Accenture researcher Jim Wilson and his colleagues have written that new jobs created by AI will fall into three categories: trainers, explainers, and sustainers.[20] Trainers will train cognitive technologies in capabilities that don't come naturally to them, for example, in empathy. Explainers, of course, explain the process and results of AI-based decisions, particularly to nontechnical senior executives. And sustainers ensure that cognitive systems are performing well over time, in areas like task performance as well as ethical compliance. The authors argue that some of these jobs will be in high demand, so organizations should begin to redesign their talent management processes to hire or train them. Wilson and Accenture Chief Technology Officer Paul Daugherty have recently written a book called *Human+Machine*[21] that identifies six hybrid roles that humans and machines will need to perform in collaboration.

This is a compelling set of arguments suggesting that augmentation is a more likely outcome than large-scale job loss from automation. Of course, that doesn't mean that in some settings companies will not replace workers with machines. Nobody knows for sure what will happen to jobs in the future, but if there is any doubt in the matter, workers with jobs, and many managers as well, will be better off if we believe in augmentation and do our best to make it effective. In the next section I will discuss some steps that can move us in that direction.

Moving Forward with Augmentation—or Automation

Whatever an organization has decided in terms of automation or augmentation as the most likely or most desirable (or both) future for its jobs, there are still many things it needs to do to move ahead with this objective. It's unlikely that one overall strategy or set of approaches will serve equally for every job. Therefore, organizations need to classify their jobs, determine the appropriate level of human and machine activity for each, identify the skills most likely to be needed in the future, and begin preparing both the people and machines for their future roles.

Classifying Jobs

Both augmentation and automation happen task by task, job by job. So it's important to identify some of the important jobs in your organization—ideally even some jobs that don't exist today—and begin to classify them in terms of the types of AI that might come into play with them. Some forward-looking companies are beginning to do this. GE, for example, has created a series of job "personas" (with, e.g., names and descriptions) that include both jobs that will largely be automated, jobs that will be substantially changed, and entirely new jobs that will be created—all specifically in reference to cognitive technology–driven change.

These personas are beginning to be used to help current employees think about how their skills need to evolve. A materials manager in a manufacturing plant, for example, needs to ensure that there are materials and components available to build or service products. In the past he or she might have automatically ordered parts based on a one-hundred-day lead time, but a machine learning model might show that some parts typically arrive in ninety days. The short-run focus will be to help the materials manager understand the statistics and make the right decision about ordering. In the future, the machine might place the order, but the materials manager will need to know why the order was placed and what assumptions are behind the machine learning analysis—and intervene when necessary.

I have identified five alternative steps that organizations can take with respect to automation.[22] These could also be used as a way to classify jobs in terms of which approach seems most likely or feasible. The five steps, which have been applied to a number of specific jobs, include:

Step In

Perhaps the most common augmentation role is *stepping in*. Those who play this role monitor and modify the work of a smart machine, and intervene when it has problems. Taxes may increasingly be done by computer, but smart tax accountants know the mistakes that automated programs often make (and the common mistakes of the human users of such programs), and look out for them. Ad buying in digital marketing is almost exclusively automated today, but only people can say when some act of "programmatic" ad buying actually hurts the brand, and how the logic behind it might be tuned. The human is ensuring that the computer is doing a good job and making it better.

Step Up

Stepping up involves adopting a managerial work design role that oversees the application of cognitive tools to the business. There will always be some jobs for people capable of more big-picture thinking and a higher level of abstraction than computers are capable of. In essence this is acting on the same advice that has always been offered and taken as automation encroaches on human work: Let the machine do the work that is beneath you, and take the opportunity that affords you to engage with higher-order concerns. People in this job need to stay broadly informed and creative enough to be part of their organization's ongoing innovation and strategy efforts.

Step Aside

Stepping aside means creating jobs out of non-codifiable human strengths that aren't about purely rational cognition, but draw on what Howard Gardner has called our "other intelligences." These jobs might focus specifically on the "interpersonal" and "intrapersonal" intelligences—knowing how to work well with other people, and understanding your own interests, goals, and strengths—or the "visual-spatial" or "bodily kinesthetic" ones involving art or physical activity.

Step Narrowly

Stepping narrowly means finding a specialty area within your profession that is so narrow that no one would be tempted to automate it; it just isn't economical to do so. These types of workers excel on the basis of their nonautomated expertise, but they can improve their performance by building their own databases and routines for keeping current, and by connecting with systems that combine the output of their very specialized work with others'.

Step Forward

Finally, to *step forward* is to construct the next generation of AI tools and software. Behind every great machine, it's still true that there is a human—often many of them. Clearly this is a realm in which knowledge workers need strong skills in computer science, artificial intelligence, and analytics. Stepping forward means bringing about the next level of encroachment of the machines, but it also is work that is itself highly augmented by hardware and software.

Of course, if one is classifying jobs or workers for the purposes of automating them away, "stepping out" of the workforce might be an additional category. My focus is on augmentation, so I do not discuss that here.

It may seem overwhelming to apply such classifications or persona development to every job in a company, but it's more feasible to do it for a subset of jobs. The subset might be based on an assessment of which jobs are most important to a company's strategy, which jobs have the most people working within them, which jobs are most subject to automation, or which jobs are deemed most likely to benefit from the addition of some AI capabilities.

One property and casualty insurance company, for example, decided that the two most important jobs to analyze with regard to AI were underwriters, who set prices for insurance, and claims adjusters. Both are well-paid, knowledge work jobs with a relatively high number of incumbents in them. The company's technologists believed that the time was ripe for revisiting the systems used to support underwriting, which were based on codified decision rule engines created in the 1990s. On further examination, however, the company found that the underwriting systems were still quite accurate. There is the potential for using sensors, satellite imagery, and other external data sources for underwriting, but the company doesn't believe that the technology and data environment is quite ready yet for this sort of application. So any major changes in the underwriting job were postponed until a later time.

For the claims adjuster job, the company has maintained a number of people scattered around the country to assess damage to cars and validate claims. However, the company has some pilots—successful thus far—involving the use of deep learning of digital images to evaluate automobile damage. The company has decided that it will need fewer claims adjusters in the near future, so it is not hiring new ones (and many of the current group of them are nearing retirement age). The claims adjustment process will eventually be almost completely centralized, with any remaining local claims work given to consultants. Claims adjusters of the future won't need to be deep learning experts, but they will need to understand how the systems make decisions and be able to communicate effectively about them with customers and agents.

For each job or each job on which the organization has decided to focus, it may also be useful to classify the appropriate and likely level of technology support. It's possible, for example, to use the autonomous vehicle six-level autonomy classification for job classification purposes. It specifies:

- Level 0—no assistance from technology
- Level 1—human assistance from technology
- Level 2—partial automation
- Level 3—conditional automation
- Level 4—high automation
- Level 5—full automation[23]

A simpler version from consultant Anand Rao divides the types of AI technology into three categories with regard to their automation objective:

• Assisted intelligence, now widely available, improves what people and organizations are already doing
• Augmented intelligence, emerging today, enables organizations and people to do things they couldn't otherwise do
• Autonomous intelligence, being developed for the future, creates and deploys machines that act on their own[24]

An organization could identify for each analyzed job the type of intelligence or automation level that is most likely to be applicable, and the rough time frame in which it will be feasible.

Once jobs have been classified in terms of the desired or likely level of automation, the next step would be to inform the incumbents of those jobs what is likely to happen and what they can do about it. If the job is to be phased out because of automation, employees could be encouraged to look or train for other jobs. If some form of augmentation is deemed likely, the focus would shift to preparing for job and skill change. In either case, employees need considerable time to adjust or retrain themselves. It's probably better to warn them too early rather than too late.

Job and Skill Change

The speed with which organizational and job changes will happen, the actual number of jobs lost, the fate of specific jobs—all of these are still very uncertain despite many predictions. What is certain is that jobs and skills will change, sometimes dramatically, as smart machines are adopted in the workplace.

Of course, some types of jobs will change more than others. The ones that will change the most include:

• *Jobs with a high degree of structure and repeatability*—Technologies like process and physical robots mean that those jobs in which key tasks are predictable and repeated often will be at risk. In factories these types of jobs have often already been replaced by robots, but now robotic process automation may substitute for human workers doing repetitive, structured tasks in offices.

• *Digital jobs that don't involve direct contact with customers*—Human customers often prefer to be dealt with by other humans. If a job doesn't involve direct contact with humans, it's more likely to be at risk. For example, in medicine, radiologists and pathologists, who don't typically see patients directly but view images of them, have more job risk than general practitioners or nurses. Offshore workers' jobs are also at risk, in part because they don't normally work in proximity to their customers or suppliers.

• *Jobs that make heavy use of quantifiable data or codifiable knowledge*—Jobs involving decisions made with data or structured, codifiable knowledge are typically more at risk than those involving knowledge or perception that varies too much to be codified. The more data involved, the more likely that machine learning algorithms can make the decision faster and more accurately than a human. Digital marketing is a great example; there is no way that a human could analyze all the necessary data and make a decision about which ad to publish on which site in less than a second.

• *Entry-level jobs*—Automation technologies have already had a negative impact on the ability of entry-level workers to get jobs in fields like architecture and law. As AI helps machines develop more capabilities, they will spread into other fields as well. Entry-level workers by definition don't have much experience or expertise, and machines can do their jobs relatively easily. That, of course, makes it difficult for entry-level workers to gain the needed experience and ever make it to senior-level roles.

• *Jobs that don't generate revenue or profit*—Companies will be inclined to apply cognitive technologies to jobs that cost them money, rather than those that make them money. If a job is in customer service, for example, it's more likely to be replaced or augmented by a machine than one in sales.

If a particular job falls into any of these categories, it doesn't mean its incumbents will be out on the street anytime soon. However, it does mean that these jobholders have a particular need to follow the capabilities of cognitive technologies, learn new skills, and be prepared to add value to what machines do.

Skills for the Future of Jobs

The skills that a particular jobholder will need to do battle with machines in the workplace—or at least complement them—will, of course, vary by the job. But some generic skills will be broadly valuable in the workforce as managers seek to maximize the value of human talent. Managers themselves will also benefit from acquiring many of these skills. They include:

• *Being conversant with how machines think*—Knowing the logic and flow of a computer system is important for anyone who works alongside or who oversees smart machines. Acquaintance with how systems think can be helpful in troubleshooting, understanding limitations, and explaining the operation of cognitive technologies. With some cognitive technologies, as in rule-based systems or robotic process automation, figuring out how a system thinks is relatively easy—the logic is transparent and accessible, even to amateurs. In the case of complex algorithmic systems like deep learning, it is much more difficult and may be impossible.

• *Having an understanding of analytics and data structures*—In the great majority of cases and types, cognitive technologies are based on analytics and data—sometimes very large volumes of it. Understanding statistics, data structures, and how to make decisions from them will be of help to anyone seeking to work with AI.

• *Becoming familiar with different types of AI*—Particularly for those individuals who seek managerial roles relative to cognitive technologies, understanding the different types and functions of the AI world is essential. It's impossible for someone to sponsor and implement a project involving image recognition, for example, if they don't know that deep learning is the most likely method to doing a good job of it.[25]

• *Having domain knowledge of the business and industry*—Anyone who wants to work alongside smart machines in a business will need to understand not only the machines themselves, but also the aspects of

the business to which they are applied. AI can't be applied to account-
ing and auditing processes, for example, without a deep understanding
of the key issues, tasks, and knowledge involved in those fields.

• *Possessing a strong ability to communicate*—As machines take on more
decisions and actions, one of the key tasks left for human workers is
effectively communicating the outcomes of machine activities to other
humans. Some insurance underwriters, for example, no longer price
insurance policies, but they work with customers and agents to communicate and justify what automated underwriting systems have decided.

• *Having high levels of emotional intelligence*—Despite some progress,
computer systems still don't possess much emotional intelligence. That
means humans have a competitive advantage in the workplace if they are
perceptive, sensitive, and insightful about human emotions. In health
care, for example, "bedside manner" will become an even more important attribute for humans seeking work in the field than it is today.

Note that I haven't put coding, or the ability to develop computer
programs, on the list. That skill would be very useful, of course, for anyone wanting to "step forward" and develop new cognitive systems. And
rudimentary coding skills are useful in learning how smart machines
think. However, many experts believe it is likely that much coding will
be automated over the next several years.[26] Therefore, developing coding skills may not be necessary for many people who want to work
alongside cognitive technologies.

Of course, the most generic skills of all are lifelong learning and
intellectual curiosity. Whatever skills and knowledge we happen to
have accumulated, chances are good that many of those intellectual
assets will no longer be relevant to an AI-driven future. We're in for a
lot of change, and that means organizations and individuals need to
learn continuously.

Bob Kegan, a professor of adult learning at the Harvard Graduate
School of Education, emphasizes this need:

The time it takes for people's skills to become irrelevant will shrink. It used to
be, "I got my skills in my 20s; I can hang on until 60." It's not going to be like
that anymore. We're going to live in an era of people finding their skills irrelevant at age 45, 40, 35.[27]

It's also clear that information technology will be key factor driving these changes, so the learning will need to have the technology at the center of it.

Company and Job-Specific Skills Strategies

I've described generic skills that may be useful for working with cognitive technologies, but companies will need to develop more detailed strategies for their organizations and for specific jobs within them.

Bank of America, for example, is automating many activities in its bank branches, so its tellers (now known as customer service representatives) are having to adopt several new skills. Since branches are largely automated, interactions with service providers will primarily be remote, oriented to specific products (e.g., mortgages) and will involve discussions of issues with self-service banking applications. A "digital ambassador" within some branches will help customers with digital banking issues and will direct them to the self-service applications they need (including Erica, the bank's digital chatbot). In other words, some tellers/CSRs will have to have deep product skills and be familiar with product-oriented applications, while others will need to be familiar with a broad range of digital banking options and have strong interpersonal skills.[28]

Jobs involving the provision of services to employees (such as IT help desks and employee onboarding) will also change with AI. Companies like ServiceNow, which already provided systems to automate key aspects of these activities, are beginning to use machine learning to add more intelligence to the processes. Since relatively simple tasks will be increasingly automated, employees in service functions will have to focus on detailed and complex service problems, and will perhaps have to specialize to gain the relevant deep knowledge. Some of the same types of changes may also be necessary for call center workers who provide services to customers.

Many jobs over the past several years have been devoted to fraud and threat detection in financial services and cybersecurity. But fraudsters and hackers have become more numerous and productive, and it is increasingly difficult to keep up with all the threats in these areas without some degree of automation.

In these roles fraud prevention and security professionals have been trained to identify threats using various data sources and signals, and then to investigate them. But as cognitive technologies increasingly perform threat detection activities, the emphasis for humans in these processes will shift toward investigation and confirmation of threats. For internal threats from employees, skills will need to shift to investigatory capabilities—interviewing, evidence-gathering, and the like—as well as legal and regulatory knowledge for human resource management. For external threats, skills may need to gravitate toward working with law enforcement agencies.

It's Time to Get Started

While the need for new skills and training related to AI may seem to be in the distant future, the time for companies to get started on these kinds of programs is now. New skills take a long time to acquire, and even developing the programs to create them can be time-consuming. Some companies appear to already be offering programs to retrain for AI-oriented skills, although I have observed few of these in practice. But in the 2017 Deloitte "cognitive aware" survey, respondents both expressed a high need for retraining and said they were already doing it.

When asked about the steps necessary to prepare employees for cognitive technologies, substantial majorities agree that most of the interventions listed were needed, including:

• Training employees to develop cognitive technologies (70 percent)
• Training employees to work alongside cognitive technologies (64 percent)
• Conducting awareness education on cognitive technologies and their implications (63 percent)
• Creating new departments and roles to lead the use of these technologies (61 percent)

Thirty-nine percent of respondents felt the need to prepare employees for alternative careers outside the company.

The perceived need for training didn't surprise me. However, given earlier results in the survey that de-emphasized automation-related job loss, I was somewhat surprised that almost two in five respondents thought retraining for alternative careers was in order. Perhaps this means that job markets in the future will be in a lot of flux, with new skill requirements and a lot of people both leaving and entering organizations.

I also did not expect that 63 percent of respondents (and 76 percent of those from companies with over 5,000 and fewer than 10,000 employees) said they already had training programs underway to prepare employees to deal with change in their jobs from cognitive technologies. Thirty-two percent said they didn't have them yet but planned to create some.

A 2017 Genpact survey of 300 global business leaders to which I have previously referred was perhaps somewhat more realistic, with lower numbers saying they are already undertaking AI-related retraining. It found that although 82 percent of the respondents plan to implement AI-related technologies in the next three years, and 57 percent believe they are likely to transform the workforce, 38 percent say they currently provide employees with reskilling options.[29]

Even the 38 percent figure seems high to me, however. I have not observed many of these AI-related retraining programs in companies. Perhaps the respondents in these surveys interpreted the survey question loosely and are saying that they do have retraining programs, albeit not driven specifically by AI.

Whether that many retraining programs are actually underway to this degree, it's not unreasonable to start them well ahead of the widespread application of cognitive technologies to your business. Such programs can be designed to yield new skills that are highly likely to be relevant to new tasks and business processes, and they signal to employees that change is coming. They are likely to motivate sentient workers to assess their own skills, to think about their futures as colleagues of cognitive machines, and to begin developing the skills that will make them successful.

7   Technical Approaches to Cognitive Technologies

I'm always wary of writing book chapters about new technology. In my previous books where I've done that, the technology chapters have always been the first to become obsolete. This is particularly problematic for the field of cognitive technologies now, when many vendors are embracing the capabilities, and startups are trying to innovate at a furious pace.

But managers still need guidance in making technology decisions about AI. I will attempt in this chapter to focus on some relatively timeless issues, such as whether a company should "build or buy" the relevant tools. However, if you are reading this book ten years after the publication date, you may want to skip this chapter in favor of a more contemporary source.

Technology Challenges

Before discussing the strategies that companies have adopted to solve the technical challenges of AI, it may be useful to describe the challenges they face. I have already mentioned in chapter 3 that integration with existing systems and business processes was the #1 challenge mentioned in the 2017 Deloitte "cognitive aware" survey (see figure 7.1). Forty-seven percent of respondents identified it as a challenge. But there are others as well. Two in five thought the technologies, or the people who can use them, were too expensive. Almost as many were challenged by the lack of understanding of managers within their organizations of cognitive technologies. About a third faced issues finding

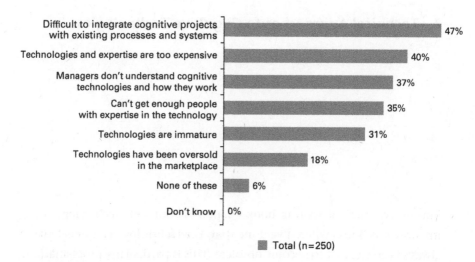

Figure 7.1
Challenges Encountered with AI/Cognitive Technologies
Source: 2017 Deloitte "Cognitive Aware" Survey

people who have sufficient cognitive expertise, and roughly the same percentage felt the technologies were immature. A relatively low percentage felt that the technologies had been oversold in the marketplace (by vendors and media, presumably). But in another question in the survey, only 9 percent agreed that "AI is over-hyped," and 10 percent felt it was "under-hyped!"

In another 2017 survey conducted by Teradata, some of the challenges were somewhat different. These were phrased as anticipated barriers to adoption, rather than challenges faced already. The survey report describes the challenges:

Almost all respondents (91 percent) anticipate significant barriers to adoption. The majority predict roadblocks due to lack of IT infrastructure (40 percent), followed by a lack of in-house talent (34 percent). Just as many, 33 percent, claim that AI technology available today is too unproven and nascent, while 30 percent yearn for more budget. However, skepticism is lower in other areas—only 19 percent are concerned that AI has a weak business case, and only 20 percent worry about the impact of AI and automation on jobs and employee morale.[1]

The "IT infrastructure" referenced in that survey, which was cited more often than any other barrier, could refer to the fact that AI hardware and software don't always mix easily with enterprise technologies. This is particularly true when AI models are developed using standalone technologies, and then have to be deployed within existing systems. As I describe later in this chapter, however, it's sometimes possible to acquire AI capabilities that are already integrated with core business software. And certain types of AI applications—notably deep learning—run best on graphics processing units (GPUs) that are not commonly used for business applications. Some businesses may have difficulty incorporating them into their hardware infrastructures, although GPU-based processing is also available in the cloud from several established vendors.

I have certainly heard other challenges mentioned in companies. Many have issues with their data—not enough of it to undertake serious AI work, or data that is of poor quality. I'll describe some efforts to address that issue later in the chapter. Related somewhat to the managerial understanding issue, some people who do cognitive technology development claim that uninformed managers push inappropriate solutions upon them because of influence from vendors (though this problem seems to be easing over time). And perhaps related to the expense issue, there are many complaints that companies aren't investing enough. In another question on the Deloitte survey, 92 percent agreed strongly or agreed that "my company would innovate more effectively if we invested more in AI/cognitive technologies." In the Teradata survey, however, only 30 percent of respondents believed that their organization wasn't investing enough to keep up with industry competitors.

I can't solve all those problems in this chapter, but I do provide approaches to several of them.

Developing a Technology Strategy for AI

What technologies should an organization acquire or develop in order to meet its objectives with cognitive technology? How should it adopt and implement them? Those are complicated questions that are important for organizations to answer. As I've discussed, cognitive technology is not one technology, but a collection of them, so picking and implementing the technologies that solve your organization's business problems are key tasks. Beyond the choice of technologies, companies need to decide whether to build or buy the technology capabilities, whether to use proprietary or open source software, whether to use a single vendor's tools or employ "best of breed," whether to use a broad "platform" or single applications, and so on.

There are no right answers to these questions—only a set of answers that fit or don't fit the organization's capabilities, business strategy, and other aspects of its cognitive strategy. Some sets of matches between particular technologies and business problems are likely to be better than others, however.[2] A full mapping is beyond the scope of this chapter, but if, for example, your organization has voluminous and rapidly changing but structured (i.e., in rows and columns of numbers) data about customers, machine learning will probably provide a better understanding of their preferences. If you have images to identify, deep learning neural networks are likely to be the best bet—and so on.

In order to make such technology decisions, an organization needs not only a clear idea of what business objectives it wants to accomplish, but also what specific methods it needs to use to solve them. There are, for example, hundreds of algorithms to choose from in machine learning, and not all software includes all algorithms. There are multiple approaches to natural language processing, including the two general classes of statistical NLP and semantic NLP. Even robotic process automation, the least intelligent of all cognitive software types, has various capabilities for supporting business functions and for learning, depending on the vendor and software. In order to ascertain the right technology to build or buy, a company needs to involve not only executives but also expert analysts, IT professionals, and data scientists.

A key factor in all technology decisions is the level of expertise and sophistication of the organization with cognitive technology. Sophisticated companies have many different choices to make than those just getting started. Take, for example, Procter & Gamble and American Express. These two firms have been working—on and off—with artificial intelligence since the 1980s (primarily with "expert system" rule-based technologies). With their levels of experience and expertise, they can:

• Build their own cognitive applications, rather than buying them from vendors

• Manage a collection of disparate cognitive tools, rather than an integrated "platform"

• Develop applications with open-source tools

• Use their own internal developers and data scientists rather than external contractors

These approaches have worked well for companies like P&G and AmEx, but would not be a great fit for those that don't have such a high level of sophistication and experience with the technology. Even if firms were able to employ them with the help of external consultants or vendors, they would need to build their own capabilities over time.

In the next section I'll describe some strategies for implementing cognitive technologies within your company ranked according to their difficulty and requirements for technical sophistication—starting with the easiest approach.

Implementing Cognitive Capabilities from Transaction Software Vendors

One of the easiest ways for your organization to enter the world of cognitive technologies is to employ the cognitive capabilities that mainstream business application vendors are embedding into their applications. These are typically transactional systems for things like customer relationship, supply chain, or human resource management—all of which can benefit from greater intelligence.

Most companies have these systems installed already, and the need for them isn't going away. Adding intelligence can mean that instead of reporting what transactions have happened, the systems could tell people how to do their jobs more effectively. They might automatically recommend, for example, what customers to call on, how much inventory should be in the supply chain, and which employees are at risk of leaving. It is normally much easier to have such intelligence embedded within a system that your people already use, rather than having them go through a separate application and the steps to use it. And in many cases the needed data for cognitive analyses is already resident in the transactional system.

I won't do a detailed review of the options for this approach, since they are changing all the time. But Salesforce.com has been one of the earliest vendors to employ it, so I will discuss that company's approach in some detail (disclosure: I occasionally deliver presentations to customers for Salesforce). Einstein, Salesforce's umbrella term for AI capabilities, embeds several cognitive and analytical functions into its customer relationship management applications. The company says that more than twenty Einstein features are included in all of its "clouds" for sales, marketing, service, e-commerce, and community. Some of the Einstein functions include predictive lead scoring and prioritization, automating data entry, ad personalization, social media and email sentiment analysis, personalized product recommendations, and image classification. In analytics, Einstein Discovery finds patterns in data without requiring human hypotheses.

Some companies have already begun to use these capabilities.[3] U.S. Bank, for example, used Einstein's predictive lead scoring capabilities, which rely on machine learning, to identify customers who were likely to need wealth management capabilities. The company achieved 2.34 times the number of conversions from the scoring approach. The Finnish elevator/escalator company Kone is using Einstein in the Salesforce service cloud to identify the best service technician to solve a customer's problem before dispatching them. The outdoor equipment company Black Diamond says that Einstein's automated product recommendations increased its conversions by about 10 percent and its revenues per website visit by 15 percent. It's still early days for these capabilities, but they appear to be providing value already and are relatively easy to implement, at least from a technical perspective.

SAP, Oracle, and Workday are also embedding cognitive technologies into their enterprise resource planning systems. Some of the functions they offer are similar to those of Salesforce, such as scoring and prioritizing leads and personalizing customer content. In addition to these machine learning–based capabilities, SAP is focused on chatbot-driven "conversational commerce" and image/facial recognition. Its AI capabilities, which it collectively calls Leonardo Machine Learning, also include specific solutions like cash management in finance, video analysis in brand management, and trouble ticket analysis in customer service.[4] SAP has adopted a strategy of making available proprietary or open source AI tools in its own offerings—typically in the form of APIs that its systems can call—which I think is a good one.

Oracle has a strong focus on chatbot-like interaction with its systems and on its extensive data resources, particularly on companies. Workday is strongly focused on employee retention analysis. None of these companies is moving at the pace of Salesforce, but all appear to be working hard to integrate AI into their offerings.[5] Because they have transactional systems in place within many customers, they have a built-in advantage over startups with standalone solutions. But it's also important to mention that startups often provide integration with well-known transaction software. Conversica, for example, an "AI virtual assistant" company that creates automated messages for sales conversions, says that its software integrates easily with Salesforce and other leading CRM packages.

Robotic Process Automation as an Entry-Level Strategy

Another relatively easy entry-level strategy into cognitive technology is to employ robotic process automation tools for structured digital processes. One consultant I interviewed described it as a "gateway drug" for other cognitive technologies. RPA is easy to configure and implement, and small implementations may not even require an expert consultant or much help from a vendor. These systems do interface with existing IT applications, however, so consultation with the IT function in a company is a good idea. Ongoing "robot management and governance" is important in large-scale RPA implementations.

The greatest RPA strength and the greatest shortcoming is that it doesn't change the underlying systems to which it connects or the process tasks it automates. This is the key to its easy implementation, but it limits the ability to simplify the processes and to modify the underlying systems architecture. In a sense RPA is pouring cement—albeit quick-set cement—around existing systems. Its simple architecture also limits the ability to create and act on intelligence.

Perhaps the key shortcoming of RPA today is that it is simply not very smart. RPA as of now doesn't have much capability to eliminate unneeded process steps, create intelligence, learn, or act intelligently. It is possible that vendors will add intelligence to RPA over time. Already some vendors have incorporated a limited capability to "observe" human coworkers and take similar actions. Some vendors are trying to create chatbot interfaces to RPA robots. One leading RPA vendor, Blue Prism, recently announced that it was partnering with IBM and other vendors with the goal of adding intelligence to its RPA offerings. Another, UIPath, says it already has some machine vision capabilities. Work-Fusion, an RPA company that focuses on financial process automation, combines RPA with machine learning and chatbots in many applica-tions. Another leading RPA vendor, Automation Anywhere, offers fairly strong analytical and reporting functions. IPsoft's Amelia is primarily an intelligent agent, but it does also have some RPA capabilities.

What would it mean to have an intelligent RPA solution? In effective digital organizations, smart machines should be able to:

• *Eliminate process steps or processes*—Intelligent process robots could per-form complex tasks and altogether eliminate the routine steps performed by humans, for example, automatically gathering and computing data from multiple sources.

• *Create intelligence*—Smart RPA systems would be able to create intel-ligence through interpretation of structured and unstructured infor-mation, and facilitate decision making based on the information. For example, an automation solution for the "front desk" in the insurance industry should be able to interpret and extract key information from submissions, contracts, and invoices, prioritize them for underwriting, and automatically reconcile them with claims for a cost audit.

• *Learn*—Intelligence would also mean learning from past perfor-mance and human behavior to automate exception cases. Smart machines should also be able to learn from structured and unstructured information to identify new patterns/intelligence. For example, they could develop intelligence about customer preferences from emails, CRM notes, attachments, and so forth. Ideally they would know why a customer is contacting an organization.

• *Act intelligently*—Smart RPA could automate certain tasks based on the intelligence created by the machine. In an order fulfillment process, for example, it should be able to determine whether a delivery truck should be at the warehouse or not. It could also compare the truck plate number with the order management system and send a signal to open the warehouse gate.

• *Perceive its environment*—RPA systems with intelligence should be able to perform machine vision, take orders in human speech, and so forth.

At least some of these components of process robotic intelligence have already emerged, and more are likely to come over the next several years. That makes RPA a reasonable entry-level approach to AI even most implementations of the technology are not very smart today.

Implementing a Broad Cognitive Platform with Vendor Help

Companies without much experience but with a desire to build a lot of cognitive applications may want to employ a cognitive "platform" with a variety of different tools. In the 2017 Deloitte "cognitive aware" survey, 20 percent of respondents said they worked primarily with one vendor of AI capabilities—which may mean a platform (see figure 7.2). IBM's Watson is perhaps the best-known example of such a platform; it has a variety (now 16, though the number has gone up and down throughout Watson's history) of component APIs that can be assembled in various ways.

The strength of a platform is that a company can create multiple cognitive applications with tools from one vendor and some degree of common user interface. The downside, as a recent investment report from Jeffries[6] described in the case of Watson, is the need for extensive consulting services to configure and integrate all the components. Many early adopters of platforms have found these services to be quite expensive.

Some other platforms in addition to Watson are beginning to emerge, although few can match its broad capabilities. Cognitive Scale, for example, has two classes of applications, one to "engage" customers through personalized content and online experiences, and the other to "amplify" employee intelligence with a knowledge management-like solution—both on a common platform. RAGE Frameworks, recently acquired by Genpact, has a series of eighteen "intelligent machines" to perform cognitive tasks in a broader context of information systems to drive business processes. Veritone, a startup with roots in digital media management, has the capability to select among a variety of "engines"—some proprietary, some open source—to accomplish specific cognitive tasks, both within and across categories of cognitive technology. Their assumption is that cognitive engines will become increasingly common and commoditized, and that companies will simply turn to the one that best solves a particular problem at the time. Each of these platforms may also require integration to build a specific application.

Building Multi-Vendor and Open-Source Capabilities

As I've suggested, the most sophisticated large firms are relying not on one vendor, but on a variety of "best of breed" cognitive tools, including open source. Some, like Procter & Gamble, have a list of vendors and software that they have examined and certified for use on AI projects. This is the most difficult approach to AI technologies, but can also be the most rewarding for those companies with the ability to execute on it.

Open source tools for AI are proliferating rapidly. Google's Tensorflow is now fairly widely used for machine and deep learning applications. Microsoft offers the open source Cognitive Toolkit. Amazon has made the machine learning technology behind its recommendation engine, DSSTNE, available as an open source tool. Caffe is a deep learning framework originally developed at UC Berkeley. Torch is an open source machine learning library, originally designed for scientific computing. Cloud platforms like Amazon Web Services or Microsoft Azure typically make available a variety of open source tools. Of course, even knowing the differences between these open source tools and

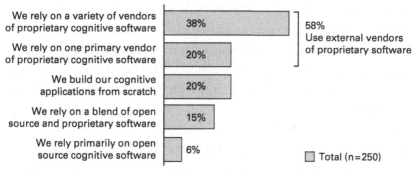

Figure 7.2
Approaches to Cognitive Software
Source: 2017 Deloitte "Cognitive Aware" Survey

when each is most appropriate requires a high level of data science sophistication.

In the 2017 Deloitte "cognitive aware" survey, 38 percent of the respondents said they relied on a variety of vendors of cognitive software (see figure 7.2). Only 6 percent relied primarily on open source tools. The most experienced and aggressive users of cognitive technology in the survey, however, were the most likely to use multiple vendors and open source software. They were also the most likely to use internal resources for development (as opposed to consultants and vendors).

Taking the multivendor, open source approach to cognitive software requires that companies be very familiar with the different types of cognitive technologies, that they have sophisticated data scientists on staff, and that they are willing to expend considerable effort on integration with existing processes and systems. As I have noted, more survey respondents identified such integration as a challenge for their organizations than any other issue. However, I believe that this approach is the way to get the highest level of technical capabilities.

Established firms with a lot of legacy software may also find that they can often rely on existing components of their technology "stack" for cognitive work. In the case of statistical machine learning and neural networks, firms may already have some of the capabilities they need if they previously implemented statistical and analytical "packages" from companies like SAS and IBM's SPSS. Machine learning and neural network analysis have been available, for example, in the SAS Enterprise Miner product for over twenty years. It is also possible to build deep learning models with SAS technology. If your company has staff who are experienced and comfortable with these tools, that may be the best option.

In general, if firms plan to make cognitive technology a core capability that is reflected in multiple projects, processes, and products, it makes sense to build internal expertise with multiple technology offerings, both proprietary and open source. But if the cognitive application is a marginally important or one-off example, it makes sense to use as much external technology and services as necessary to implement it.

Getting Data Ready

If it's not obvious already, having good and plentiful data is a precondition for effective deployment of cognitive technologies. The availability of high-quality and high-volume data is particularly important for any machine learning-based applications. The quality issue means that data should be clean, consistent, and well-integrated throughout the organization.

This highly desirable state, however, is seldom achieved in large organizations. Companies have substantial data quality problems, many of which enter the data when a front-line worker inputs it, and there are insufficient technologies or processes to fix it at that point. They also often have many different sources of key data, either because their business units and functions have been relatively independent, or because they have acquired or merged with other organizations with different databases or data architectures from their own. Addressing this situation has always been labor intensive and time consuming, and many organizations lost patience with their data management efforts.

These problems have long been addressed primarily by top-down data management frameworks, originally referred to as *information engineering* and more recently called *master data management*. They specify what the key data entities are within an organization and their relationships with other entities. The goal of these efforts is to create a set of "golden records" that are correct and consistent across an organization. If, as is normally the case, a company finds multiple sources of data for key entities, it embarks upon a "data mastering" activity that uses rule engines to match similar data. Often, however, there is a need for many rules, and data mastering ends up not saving much time over manual matching.

AI—and machine learning in particular—has the potential to come to the rescue of these efforts, however. Mike Stonebraker—a distinguished developer of database technology over time, and winner of a recent Turing Award (computer science's equivalent of the Nobel Prize), has argued passionately that "probabilistic matching" through machine learning is far more productive than rule-based approaches.[7] Other automated or semiautomated technologies can aid the process of cataloguing data, keeping track of data provenance, and enforcing data governance rules. All of these tools are beginning to crack the problem of data management, and any company interested in using its data for AI applications should consider employing them.

Of course, data management is a huge subject in itself, and it's not the primary focus of this book (perhaps a good thing for both of us, because it's not the most exciting subject to write or read about). However, it's important to face up to the issue of good data before embarking on an ambitious initiative involving AI. I've spoken with several organizations whose IT executives were reluctant to "open the floodgates of AI" because their data simply weren't up to the task. Sometimes the organizations have also simply had other, more pressing priorities than deploying cognitive tech.

Below I will describe two organization's efforts to transform their data before embarking upon major AI programs. One company, Bank of Montreal, applied relatively traditional data management methods to create opportunities for using AI in the business. The other, GlaxoSmithKline, used AI itself to help integrate its research data. Their stories provide some context for the data transformations they have undertaken to prepare for more use of AI.

Laying the Data Groundwork at Bank of Montreal

BMO Financial Group, widely known is BMO, is based in Toronto and is one of the "big five" Canadian banks, as well as one of the ten largest in North America.[8] It has a sizable presence in the United States, having acquired Harris Bank and several others in the country.

For the last several years, BMO has initiated a series of transformations to its technology infrastructure under the leadership of Jean-Michel Arès, the group head of technology and operations, and Francois Joanette, the bank's chief data officer. As with many large banks, complying with regulatory requirements has been a top priority. The bank also needed to update its basic processes for storing and reporting on data. Data science and cognitive technologies were certainly of interest to the bank, but since they both rely heavily on large volumes of high-quality data, these new technologies needed to wait for the infrastructure improvements.

Many of the needed infrastructure improvements were in place by 2017, and BMO developed a Smart Core of data capabilities that will leverage future analytics, data science, and cognitive activity. The Smart Core encompasses provisioning of data records, reference data, data governance (seventeen governance communities across the bank), and a metadata hub. The bank has already saved over $100M in data reuse and data warehouse rationalization. The "smart" aspects of the core include a data science platform including analytics sandboxes and open source software for machine learning, as well as software for robotic process automation.

The objective of data-driven activity at BMO has begun to shift from largely defensive applications (regulatory, security, and risk) to offense-oriented ones involving customer acquisition and growth.[9] The company is focused on such projects as customer journey analysis, better management of customer leads, and unstructured customer data analysis. The bank has already achieved several times more value in additional revenues over what it has saved in data rationalization.

In terms of cognitive technologies, machine learning and robotic process automation are the primary focus of the bank. Machine learning is being used for detailed segmentation of customers as well as for fraud prevention. Robotic process automation, as in most companies, is being used to drive highly structured back-office processes involving interaction with multiple information systems. For example, the bank has implemented one RPA robot in the area of high-risk investigations; it assembles data and prioritizes cases for human intervention. Conventional RPA is being augmented by optical character recognition capabilities to turn images into text, and machine learning to read unstructured text, evaluate and approve decisions, match data across databases, and route cases to the most qualified employee.

BMO is positive about the opportunities for RPA, but Arès and Joanette believe that there are substantial implications for both IT infrastructure and business processes for many of them. In terms of infrastructure, since RPA robots act as users of multiple back-end systems, changing those systems means that the RPA systems also need to be changed. Without detailed documentation of what links to what and careful change management, the architecture could become a disaster. On the process front, RPA presents an opportunity for the bank not just to automate existing processes, but to improve them as RPA is implemented. BMO is fortunate that, unlike many companies, its current business processes are documented to a high level of detail.

These new capabilities are leading BMO executives to consider some new organizational structures for data science and cognitive technologies. Thus far, advanced analytics and cognitive-oriented professionals have largely been located in functions and business units. But as these experts become increasingly important to the bank's future, there is discussion about having more central coordination of their activity. It is unlikely there will be a fully central data science group, but data scientists in local functions may well be matrixed to the Technology and Operations group to some degree.

Arès and Joanette are modest about their deployments of advanced analytical and AI capabilities, but they have made considerable strides in setting the table for that kind of work. It's relatively easy to implement advanced applications in the research lab, but much tougher in a conservative banking context with considerable regulation and many legacy systems.

Biting the Data Bullet at GlaxoSmithKline

Many large organizations eventually realize that they don't have the data environments they need to succeed with broad-scale AI work.[10] For Glaxo-SmithKline's (GSK) Research and Development (R&D) organization, that time was in early 2015. The president (at that time) of the unit Patrick Vallance and his senior colleagues deliberated on whether their data environment was of sufficient quality and integration to use tools like machine learning to help develop new drugs. They examined not only GSK's situation, but compared it to other companies who were increasingly competing on the basis of their analytical and cognitive capabilities.

Their conclusion was that the data at GSK R&D needed a major transformation. To lead it they brought in Mark Ramsey as the first head (and senior vice president) of R&D Data. He was charged with overseeing a transformation in how data and analytics were used across the organization. Vallance and his team had a vision for data within GSK R&D, which was to make it easier to access and use for exploratory analysis and decision making about new medicines. GSK had been relatively good at making decisions with data, but the executives felt—and Ramsey quickly agreed—that the data within R&D were too siloed and fragmented to be used effectively for widespread data exploration with machine learning. In particular, R&D data were kept within silos created for particular scientists, experiments, or clinical trials. Secondary analyses were almost impossible.

To determine the extent of the problem and confirm his initial impressions, Ramsey used a survey instrument developed by the MIT International Society of Chief Data Officers (isCDO). It included questions like how easy was it to share data across the organization, whether scientists could get data from other departments, and how feasible was it to perform analytics on data across the organization. He sent it to all of the 10,000 scientists within R&D, and 30 percent—an unusually high number—responded. The survey responses were virtually unanimous that it was very difficult or impossible to work with data outside of personal or departmental siloes.

So integrating diverse data was clearly the top priority for Ramsey and his team. To guide and prioritize their activities, they identified over twenty use cases for what questions the scientists wanted to answer with R&D data, and eventually selected ten as the focus. They were judged as having the greatest value, importance to key decisions, and role in addressing important scientific questions. More broadly, the goal of the work was to provide analytics-ready data of all kinds across R&D in a timely manner.

The R&D data team also looked at what other pharma firms were up to with data in order to guide and validate their own approach. Most were focusing on "real world evidence" data from insurance claims and electronic health records. Another group was focused on clinical trial data. Yet another concentrated on DNA sequencing data. GSK was interested in all of these, but the goal was to work both within and across these data domains, rather than having each as distinct effort.

A traditional master data management approach—which typically involves a lot of top-down mapping of data sources and uses (Ramsey characterizes it as "map and move")—would have taken too much time and effort to implement. There were millions of data elements to rationalize. Ramsey knew that companies were beginning to apply big data and analytics tools. One company with tools for that purpose, Tamr, stood out for its machine learning technology and focus on the pharmaceutical industry, among other industries. Tamr's cofounder and CEO, Andy Palmer, was once global head of software and data engineering for the Novartis R&D organization. As a result, Tamr was very familiar with pharma industry data standards like CDISC (Clinical Data Interchange Standards Consortium). (As I mentioned earlier, I am an advisor to Tamr).

GSK decided to employ the "probabilistic matching" approach used by Tamr (similar to the one I described earlier at GE) to combine data across the organization into a single data lake (based on Hadoop, the popular open source program used to store big data in its original format) with three different domains. First would be "assays," or data from experiments. Second would be clinical trial data. And third would be genetic data. The goal was to get 100 percent of the data into the lake within three months—an unheard-of objective using traditional data management approaches. But GSK was able to use the tools to understand the level of duplication and pull the data together in the desired timeframe. To work across the three domains, the R&D data team created an "integrated layer" on top of them with standardized ontologies; this was the only way to solve the use cases.

In the clinical trials domain, for example, Ramsey and his colleagues believed there was a massive amount of insight possible outside of the original goals for a particular trial. But combining trial data was difficult because there is a lot of variance in how they are conducted and their results recorded. But using industry standard formats, the data (originally in GSK internal formats) were ingested and mapped to the industry standard, and machine learning models learned the process. The team would feed in the source trial data, and what the target format should look like—and then let the machine go to work. Outcomes initially had 50/60 percent accuracy levels, and now in some domains they are at 100 percent accuracy. After the models were developed and refined, they could be applied to other data with relatively little human intervention—just some occasional judgments from an expert team.

GSK uses a best-of-breed approach to deliver on the overall R&D data strategy, integrating several other technologies to deliver on the use cases. Ramsey has the vision to simplify future large-scale implementations with progress in how the technologies work together. GSK hosts partner summits with the key technology companies to ensure that collaboration is a key component of their development roadmaps.

Now that the data management bullet has been bitten (perhaps in a faster and less painful way than anticipated), GSK is beginning to see some of the benefits. Scientists are beginning to see what an asset they have now, and the number of use cases has expanded from ten to 250. Many projects that use the new data environment are underway. There are significant reductions in times to get an answer to an ad hoc question. As GSK has rationalized clinical trial data, a team is focused on "clinical trial diversity" to make sure the company's trials match the demographics of patients. Real world evidence from more than thirty sources is now rationalized to the industry standard—instead of being a catch-all category, as it is in many pharma firms. GSK is also using combined clinical trials data to reuse placebo patients where appropriate.

They can simulate the control arm in some cases rather than having to give new patients placebos.

In the genetic data domain, GSK has established a relationship with UK BioBank, which is doing full genetic sequencing on their 500,000 patients. GSK will have data not only on their genomes, but also their health records, and will be able to undertake many studies on them in the identification of new drug targets.

Ramsey feels that the data foundation has been laid, but actually building the house—that is, using the data for better science—will require help from AI. He notes:

We are doing a step change on machine learning. We're looking for "blue unicorns"—people who are life scientists and also machine learning experts. We simply have to have more machine learning skills to deal with all the available data now. We're training current scientists and also recruiting. We find that our data assets make it much easier to attract the right people.

GSK R&D's data environment is something that one often hears about in startups, but is rarely found in large enterprises whose roots go back over 300 years. And it's great news for all of us humans who will benefit from the scientific advances it is likely to engender.

Exploiting External Data

Note that several of the data initiatives underway at GSK involved external data. One major change in the data environment for AI is the increasing amount of external data—such as from governments, private sector data firms, and the internet. As one insurance executive commented to me in an email:

We are moving to a world in which analytics projects are no longer dominated by in-house data. Rather, external data (and data from value-chain partners) is starting to dominate. Today, it's 80% internal, 20% external. In the next turn of the crank for data science, these ratios will be reversed. We need the ability to rapidly combine diverse data sets to support analytics.

Data on customers and potential customers, for example, is changing rapidly. In the business to consumer (B2C) space, data integrators such as Axciom, Oracle, Neustar, and KBM iBehavior are connecting online and offline sources of data on consumers. Most of these companies make use of machine learning to match data. The integrated data can provide a much more insightful view of customers for AI applications like recommendations and content personalization.

While B2C firms have typically known more about their customers than businesses that serve other businesses, there is also an emerging capability to gain insights on business customers.[11] B2B customer insight is experiencing an intensified focus as the availability of new external data describing businesses grows. Traditional B2B insight activities have involved such limited data as size of companies as measured by revenue, capitalization or employees, and industry type as formally classified by SIC codes.

The internet and electronic platforms are facilitating the creation of new business descriptors that entail a much more detailed level of data that goes well beyond a standard industry categorization. Web content that provides robust, detailed descriptions of companies provides valuable descriptive information. However, these digital resources yield little value unless individual customers are identified and their detailed backgrounds and interests analyzed to provide strategic insights for suppliers. Machine learning algorithms provide the answer in this case.

Neural networks—both traditional and deep learning algorithms—along with other machine learning methods enable data scientists to extract important data from digital formats. These AI based methods involve advanced search techniques that identify, categorize, and gather user-defined data elements corresponding to search criteria. For example, considerable business description information exists on LinkedIn, but it was historically difficult to extract and add to company profiles. Well-designed AI algorithms are the key to extracting key information elements from LinkedIn. These more structured data resources then provide the platform for yet another application of AI based algorithms, where the focus is on identifying patterns in data that ultimately provide the basis for predictive sales and marketing models. These can be used for scoring, forecasting, and classification capabilities.

One vendor focusing on AI based analytics for B2B applications leverages the extensive digital footprints that provide descriptive attributes of all types of firms. EverString Technology crawls across the diverse sectors of the web that contain descriptive information of businesses (e.g., site domains and employee digital footprints) and also incorporates input from expert practitioners in the B2B space to help further describe individual businesses. EverString deploys AI based methods including neural network and machine learning techniques to identify, extract, and model a categorization scheme of companies so that users in the B2B space can more accurately identify opportunities.

B2B companies need to know, for example, how many companies exist in a given market space, as well as the specific buyers they should target within those firms. By creating a micro-categorization scheme from applying guided AI to various sectors of the web, EverString can produce thousands of customer insights to augment customer data in a short period for their B2B customers.

One B2B company that uses EverString's platform is Autodesk, a multinational software company that provides software for the architectural, engineering, construction, manufacturing, media, and entertainment industries. A major focus in Autodesk's approaches to B2B sales over the past several years has been on using more data for account selection and understanding. But in large design-oriented companies, it is often difficult to understand which individuals might have an interest in computer-aided design (CAD) software.

Prior to working with EverString, Autodesk relied on field experience and customer buying histories. Now they rely increasingly on predictive analytics from EverString to identify likely customers. One key model is the Enterprise Business Agreement Propensity Model, which suggests which executives within a large customer organization are most likely to engage in an enterprise-level agreement with Autodesk. The company also maintains an overall account potential model that also makes use of EverString data and predictions.

The primary users of the data and models are, of course, members of the Autodesk sales force. They are given ranked recommendations and also the raw scores created by the EverString models. The Global Sales Strategy organization within Autodesk manages the process and tries to ensure that the data and models check out.

It is early days for the use of these capabilities at Autodesk, but thus far both the sales teams and the Global Sales Strategy group feel that the EverString offerings are very helpful to the sales process. As Matthew Stevens, Autodesk's sales insights manager within Global Sales Strategy put it:

EverString provides key inputs on analytics, which we convert into potential sales opportunities. It's early to judge the exact payoff, but it's difficult to imagine making a recommendation without these insights. We are challenged to respond to all the questions about accounts and scores, but at least we have data to support our recommendations now.

Stevens also noted that there are many more activities to pursue in the future with this data-driven approach to sales:

Finding data on European and Asian companies is challenging due to privacy regulations and language differences. We're working with EverString to understand these opportunities better. Currently our EverString analytics and data are not connected with Salesforce, our CRM system. But we are at the first stage of a multistage journey to understand analytics and insights in sales. We are definitely moving in the right direction.

New tools from organizations like EverString are enabling B2B-oriented firms like Autodesk to develop much more data-driven approaches to sales and marketing. The amount and quality of external data on businesses may not yet approach that for consumers, but there is considerable progress being made in achieving parity.

There is an explosion of external data already available, but it is only beginning. The rise of sensor data from the Internet of Things, smart grids in utilities, autonomous vehicle data, and many other sources will make what is available today look paltry. Only AI will be able to address data of this volume and frequency. It is not coincidental that AI is rising at the same time this flood of data is appearing.

8 Managing the Organizational, Social, and Ethical Implications of AI

It is widely agreed that there are profound implications for organizations and societies from artificial intelligence. I've already discussed some of the employment issues that may arise from advances in AI. In addition to those, many observers have begun to comment on the various social and ethical issues that may come to the fore as AI becomes more intelligent and more widely adopted.

Some possible roles of governments with regard to these issues have been widely discussed. Alternative actions by governments might include establishing training programs, providing "minimum basic incomes" or guaranteed jobs for workers displaced by AI, or even taxing robots. None of these programs has yet been adopted on a full-scale basis by any government, but at least there is discussion (and in some cases, pilot programs) of them.

But what is the perspective of businesses on these topics? What is the responsibility of companies to prevent or address the negative impacts of cognitive technologies, and to encourage the positive ones? These questions have been much less widely discussed, and I'll focus on them in this chapter. I have already discussed the job loss issue at considerable length in chapter 6 (and in the book *Only Humans Need Apply*), so I will only touch briefly on it in this chapter.

In this chapter I will primarily focus on problems related to AI and the possibility of preventing them. Like most technologies, AI has the potential to both cause and solve problems. Most accounts focus on only one or the other effect. A recent report authored by twenty-six academics, for example, focuses on the malicious use of AI, particularly in hacking, other crimes, and the military.[1]

But it is important for all of us to remember that AI and related technologies offer enormous potential for good, and they have already accomplished some of it. In a broad variety of social domains—healthcare, law enforcement, transportation, agriculture, and many types of businesses—AI is improving performance and productivity, and people are benefitting from the changes it engenders. The challenges and social dysfunctions created by AI have some possible solutions, which I will discuss, and many potential challenges have yet to occur. Talking about challenges before they arise can ensure that we have effective solutions in place when we need them.

Perhaps the most important issue for businesses with regard to AI is to avoid doing any harm to the societies and economies in which they operate. Because of the uncertainties and fast-changing technology of artificial intelligence, it may be difficult to anticipate all sources of harm in advance—although certainly companies should try to do so. But when signs of harm appear, it's important to acknowledge and act on them quickly. It's also important for companies to create small-scale experiments whenever possible to learn about potentially negative outcomes before they happen on a broad scale.

So this is just the time to begin thinking about negative AI consequences. Since it's early days for AI, many of the negative outcomes have largely appeared in research exercises or games. However, these exploratory results do illustrate some possibilities to be avoided and possible interventions. For example, in one research exercise, Google's Deepmind played a fruit-gathering game against another version of itself, and displayed some aggressive and selfish behaviors when fruit became scarce.[2] The Google researchers found that it was possible to manipulate intelligent agents to make them more or less cooperative.

Facebook's Troubles and Interventions with AI

Perhaps the single best example of recognizing and acting on harm from AI—although the final outcomes are not yet known—are at Facebook. To put it more accurately, it's not that AI is causing harm at Facebook, but that the company tried to use AI to prevent harm, and it hasn't been successful. Other social media companies have faced AI-related problems as well, but none to the degree of Facebook. The company, as I noted in chapter 1, was an early and aggressive user of AI, but its use of the technology has not always gone smoothly. The company has employed machine learning and other automation-oriented algorithms for many of its advertising functions, including suggesting ad targeting categories to potential advertisers. Those algorithms appear to be blind to racial or religious smears. In September 2017, the investigative journalism site ProPublica reported that:

it was able to use Facebook's advertising platform to target users who had expressed interest in topics such as "Jew hater" and "German Schutzstaffel," also known as the Nazi SS. And when *ProPublica*'s reporters were in the process of typing "Jew hater," Facebook's ad-targeting tool went so far as to recommend related topics such as "how to burn Jews" and "History of 'why Jews ruin the world.'"[3]

Facebook has also been criticized for allowing or facilitating high volumes of "fake news" from a variety of sources, including Russian actors trying to influence elections in the United States and Europe.[4] The company's news feeds (including "Trending Topics") have also allowed "fake news." Facebook has automated algorithms that supposedly identify fake or inappropriate news, ads or posts, but apparently they have not been up to the task.

Facebook (its CEO, Mark Zuckerberg, in particular) was slow to admit a problem with election-related news and ads. He initially dismissed as "crazy" the idea that Facebook had been manipulated in attempts to influence the 2016 U.S. presidential election. Later, however, he admitted the existence of a problem and said that Facebook was using several approaches to address it, including:

- creating technical tools for spotting fake news even before it's flagged by Facebook users
- working with third-party fact-checking groups to vet stories
- showing warnings alongside stories that have been flagged by Facebookers or third-party groups
- tweaking ad policies to discourage fake news stories linked to spam
- consulting journalists about fact-checking techniques[5]

More recently, Facebook has taken three major approaches to the
negative influence its algorithms seem to have had on society. One is
to add employees (at least 1,000 so far, with up to 10,000 coming) to
the company in order to provide more and faster human reviews of
potentially fake or problematic news, posts, and ads.[6] A second is to
refocus Facebook content on sources like family and friends in order to
increase meaningful social interaction.[7] A third is to let Facebook users
rank the credibility of news stories, which will presumably discourage
fake news.[8] Whether these and previous steps will solve some of the
social problems at Facebook is not yet clear. They have already been
piloted in some Facebook-using countries, and the company should
be credited for this experimentation. However, the steps taken in these
experiments don't appear to have solved the problems and may even
have exacerbated them.[9] Posts that are shared by family and friends
may be less likely to involve professional, objective news sources. Some
recent research out of MIT suggests that one of the reasons fake news
(on Twitter in particular) has proliferated—traveling farther, faster,
deeper and more broadly than true news—is that many people simply
prefer it or find it more interesting than the truth.[10]

Facebook's AI-related issues go beyond fake news about politics and
hate speech. Some have accused the company of encouraging suicide by
live-streaming examples of it, although it is difficult to detect and remove
such videos in real time (YouTube also struggles with this problem). Facebook has also been accused of contributing to the "filter bubble" problem, in which people only receive content that they agree with. Finally,
the company also has a large number of "fake users"—accounts for people who don't exist or are fraudulent. AI is used to try to identify such
accounts, but it has not been very successful. Facebook estimated that
there may have been as many as sixty million fake accounts in 2017.[11]

Of course, Facebook is to some degree a victim of its own success.
Surveys suggest that 40 percent of U.S. adults get their news from Facebook, and the company has over two billion users. To have human
review of all Facebook content would perhaps require much of the workforce of some large countries. The company clearly needs to continue
using machine learning and other forms of AI to review and sometimes

remove content, but it may not yet have achieved the balance of interventions to address the problems its popularity has helped to create.

Other companies involved in social media have had some problems as well with AI, but none to the degree of Facebook. In one well-known example, the Microsoft autonomous social media system Tay learned to spew out hateful messages from observing U.S. human social media comments (the Chinese version was much more polite). Tay was a research project, and it was quickly discontinued. The program published in tweets, but Twitter apparently doesn't use AI to filter inappropriate content (although it does use machine learning to rank tweets by the predicted level of interest to users). Twitter also published tweets from fake Russian accounts designed to influence voters, but AI played no role in encouraging or preventing it.

In short, the primary failing of AI in technology and the online content industry has been the inability to prevent some unfortunate tendencies in social media. The real issue is that some companies—Facebook in particular—may have relied too heavily on cognitive tools to try to prevent antisocial behaviors. AI didn't cause the problem, but it was unable to prevent it either.

AI Fairness and Algorithmic Bias

Companies should ask themselves whether the AI systems they use are fair and whether they treat all groups equally. *Algorithmic bias* means that the outcomes of some machine learning algorithms put certain groups at a disadvantage. While the creators of the algorithms may not have intended the bias or discrimination, they and their companies have an obligation to try to prevent such problems and to correct them when they are discovered. This problem is not new and has been encountered in firms using traditional analytical approaches as well.[12] AI, which can create and apply more models more quickly than traditional analytics, just exacerbates it.

One of the most frequently cited examples of algorithmic bias is the COMPAS (Correctional Offender Management Profiling for Alternative Sanctions) system used for sentencing recommendations in criminal cases. This system, which uses a relatively basic form of machine learning (it is trained on data to develop a scoring system that is then applied to new data), attempts to predict the likelihood of recidivism, and is one factor used by judges in recommending sentences for convicted offenders. It was found in a ProPublica study to predict that black defendants will have higher risks of recidivism than warranted, and to predict lower rates for white defendants than warranted.[13] Northpointe, Inc., the company that developed and markets COMPAS, argues that ProPublica's analysis is incorrect.[14]

While the firm that created COMPAS is clearly research-oriented, the debate points out a related problem to algorithmic bias—lack of transparency. For competitive reasons, Northpointe refuses to release the algorithm it uses for scoring defendants. As a result, defendants and their attorneys, judges, and observers of judicial processes are unable to fully assess this (at least partial) basis for sentencing.

At least one other sentencing algorithm has been made public, and it has even improved the likelihood of alternatives to jail.[15] Called the Public Safety Assessment, it was developed by a private foundation, and the nine factors and weights used within it are publicly available.[16] The foundation is also commissioning third-party research on the impacts of the assessment.

These developments suggest that algorithms and AI programs used for public decision-making purposes may not be well suited for creation and marketing by the private sector. At a minimum, profit-making companies would seem to have some obligations to make their algorithms public under some circumstances. As less transparent programs like deep learning neural networks become more widely employed, it may be impossible to employ them in such contexts because no one could understand how they arrived at a decision.

There are other, less dramatic examples of algorithmic bias causing some social harm. AI-based navigation programs for drivers such as Google's Waze, which take crowdsourced traffic data into account in recommending routes, may result in greater congestion in residential areas or small towns. Leonia, New Jersey, recently banned nonresident travel on several of its roads because large numbers of Waze-guided commuters were traveling through the town. Similarly, navigation programs that focus only on distance may lead drivers to take shorter but more dangerous routes.

Algorithmic bias has also been found in some approaches to credit scoring. Specifically, in countries including China, Germany, India, and Russia, companies have developed credit scoring approaches that incorporate social networks. As an *Atlantic Monthly* article exploring the issue put it:

systems that take into account the actions of people's family and friends risk assigning guilt by association, denying opportunities to someone because of who they're connected to. They can decrease a person's chance for upward mobility, based solely on the social group they find themselves in.[17]

A new social credit system in China, which will be mandatory by 2020, is likely to punish consumers for political dissent or for being in social relationships with dissenters. The algorithms for social credit in China are being developed by a variety of firms but are generally secret.[18]

Related types of algorithms are being proposed to determine whether immigrants should be admitted to the United States. Under the "extreme vetting" idea proposed by President Donald Trump, the U.S. Department of Homeland Security has requested proposals from system integrators to develop software that would determine in part whether immigrants are admitted to the country. The software would attempt to determine whether the potential immigrant posed a terrorism or security risk to the United States, or at the other extreme, would have a high "probability of becoming a positively contributing member of society."[19]

The current status of the proposed software is unknown, but fifty-four experts in AI and software development signed a letter suggesting that such an automated determination was both technically infeasible and likely to be biased in its outcomes. Any private sector firm that takes on such work is likely to be the subject of considerable controversy.

One final example of algorithmic bias involves the potential for unfair treatment in how companies assess and hire job candidates. Human hiring, of course, has long been viewed as a process subject to bias, with many instances of human recruiters and interviewers seeking out candidates who are similar to themselves. Many companies now employ algorithms to score job applicants, and critics have pointed out that they can also be biased and are generally not neutral.[20] As in other areas of business and society, the algorithms employed are usually not available for review.

At least one company, however, has developed software that specifically addresses discrimination in hiring processes. Pyrmetrics is a startup that uses performance on games to match potential hires to high performers on attributes related to high performance. An AI application scores the game play for recruits to ensure that bias factors like name, gender, skin color, age, or resume entries are considered. The startup already has over fifty enterprise customers.[21] The early success of the company suggests that many firms are anxious to find nondiscriminatory hiring approaches while still benefiting from algorithms and AI.

As these examples illustrate, ignoring the possibility of algorithmic bias may mean that an otherwise promising AI initiative goes astray. When machine learning programs (which are almost always the cognitive technology involved in algorithmic bias) work well, they can dramatically improve both the process and the results over human decision making. And since humans often bring biases to their decisions (as we now know well after two Nobel Prizes in economics have been awarded for behavioral economics), machine learning offers the possibility of a more objective and data-driven approach to decision making.

To avoid the problem of algorithmic bias, companies should undertake the following steps:

- Allow as much transparency as possible in machine learning models
- Avoid using "black box" AI technologies that can't be interpreted or explained
- Avoid introducing variables or features in models that could be construed as causing bias
- Ask external reviewers to evaluate the models in question for potential bias
- Ensure that outliers or missing data aren't introducing bias in model outcomes

- Try not to have your models optimize a single business metric or outcome
- Ensure that your technologists explore technical approaches to identify and remove bias[22]
- Examine and recalculate models frequently to avoid bias from older data

AI Transparency and Explainability

Related to the algorithmic bias issue is the important topic of transparency of AI models and the ability or inability to explain how they reach decisions. As I noted, several of the algorithmic bias examples I described might have been eased or resolved by greater transparency. In those cases, the lack of transparency was related to commercial advantage; the companies involved didn't want to release the details of their algorithms.

An even greater problem with AI, however, results from an inherent problem with some cognitive technologies. As I have suggested in other chapters, technologies like deep learning make it virtually impossible to know what features or variables in the model mean, what impact they had on the outcome, and how the model arrived at an outcome. There may be millions of variables in these models, each with no inherent meaning to human observers. You can't look, for example, at the deep learning algorithm that Google used to identify cat photos on the internet, and find the variables that detected two ears, a fuzzy face, and large eyes. We simply don't know how the model was able to identify cats.

Is this a problem? Well, not so much in applications like cat identification. Who really cares how that system does its job as long as it does it well? In fact, there are many other situations in which it doesn't matter how an algorithm does its job of prediction or classification. Digital marketing is a prominent one. If an advertiser is paying only a few cents or less for each ad placement, does it really matter how the algorithm decided which potential customer receives it? The aggregate results matter, but the process by which they are achieved doesn't.

However, there are situations in which how algorithms decide matters. Health care is one of these. Doctors and patients, for example, who are told that a deep learning algorithm has identified a likely cancer on a radiology image may wish to know the details of how it came to that conclusion. Being told that the system is 99 percent accurate may not be enough to satisfy inquiring minds when the consequences are major. Health care regulators or insurers, who may have to pay for the actions to treat the cancer, are also likely to want good explanations. But it's unclear how this is going to be resolved, since at the moment there seems to be no good way to explain how deep learning can identify likely cancers—and the technology happens to be pretty good at it.

Financial services is another industry in which transparency is critical—and not only because regulators say it is. If you are denied credit because an AI algorithm has decided that you are not worthy of it, you may wish to know why. If a bank forecloses on your mortgage because its AI algorithms have predicted that you won't pay them back, you may ask for an explanation.

As I mentioned in chapter 4 with respect to Capital One, banks and other financial firms often avoid this type of opaque algorithm, in part because they don't think regulators would approve it. Capital One is studying how to make deep learning models more transparent.

Equifax has actually made some progress in this regard, as Gil Press notes in a Forbes post.[23] He quotes Peter Maynard, the company's senior vice president of global analytics, who questions that complex neural network algorithms for credit scoring can't be made transparent:

My team decided to challenge that and find a way to make neural nets interpretable. We developed a mathematical proof that shows that we could generate a neural net solution that can be completely interpretable for regulatory purposes. Each of the inputs can map into the hidden layer of the neural network and we imposed a set of criteria that enable us to interpret the attributes coming into the final model. We stripped apart the black box so we can have an interpretable outcome. That was revolutionary, no one has ever done that before.

Maynard says that the neural net has improved the predictive ability of the model by up to 15 percent. He also says that it has led the company to make a case to regulators that credit could be safely extended to customers who wouldn't get it without these models.

Given the variation in whether transparency is important or not, companies should classify their AI projects and applications in terms of how much transparency is needed. The rationale for transparency may involve regulatory approval, performance of the model, explanation to customers, or other reasons. If some transparency is deemed necessary, companies will need to employ cognitive tools and methods that are relatively less complex. Simple machine learning algorithms are often relatively interpretable, and some systems can supply "reason codes" that describe the primary factors in a predictive or classification model. There are also methods called "rule learning" that can be used alongside some machine learning algorithms—though typically not deep learning—that can shed some light on the rules and relationships inside an analytical model.

Companies should closely follow developments in regulation and customer perception that might affect the need for transparency. In the European Union, for example, one aspect of the General Data Protection Regulation (GDPR) laws taking effect in 2018 involves the "right to an explanation"—that individuals affected by computer-based decisions have a right to know why and how the decision was made. That could significantly curtail the use of technologies like deep learning that make explanations very difficult, and could force even traditional machine learning models to explain how they work.

At Danske Bank, based in Denmark, a substantial effort in 2017 involved the use of machine learning models to predict fraud.[24] Model development itself using supervised learning was difficult, particularly given that actual incidence of fraud is relatively rare. But after developing the model and deploying a real-time scoring approach to predict the likelihood of fraud, the bank had to explain to customers why their transaction may have been rejected for possible fraud. The explanations were necessary both to build customer trust and to comply with GDPR regulations.

Danske Bank employed a method called LIME (locally interpretable model-agnostic explanations) to identify the features or variables in each case that were most important in establishing a score.[25] A money transfer, for example, might be rejected for possible fraud based on the amount of money being transferred, the country it is being transferred to, and the average monthly spending of the person doing the transfer.

These reasons could be presented to the customer if requested. LIME can also work for deep learning models for tasks like image recognition, but it is often more difficult to interpret in that context.

Privacy and Data Security

Artificial intelligence is raising the ante on privacy and data security, in part because it is capable of discovering a substantial amount of detailed personal information. Facial recognition systems, for example, can identify whether an individual was at a particular store or political rally. One researcher at Stanford used deep learning systems to estimate the probability of whether a photograph is of a gay person or a straight person, based on facial characteristics.[26] AI systems increasingly can predict your health and likelihood of hospitalization or death. Machine learning systems can handle massive amounts of detail about what we buy, watch, say on social media, and the like. Many of us would prefer that all of this information remain private.

The good news is that AI can help to address cybersecurity threats, as I will describe later. Unfortunately, AI is just as likely to be used for cyberattacks as it is for protection. Detailed analyses of AI cyberattacks are rare, but in one vendor's survey, 91 percent of U.S. cybersecurity professionals are concerned that hackers will use AI to attack their companies.[27] There are predictions that hackers and cybersecurity professionals may soon engage in an AI-fueled arms race.[28]

On the cybersecurity protection side, the primary use of cognitive tools thus far is to address the skill shortage of cybersecurity professionals. The explosion of cyberattacks and security breaches has led to a widely discussed shortage of such skills, and AI can help to make up the difference. The most common approach is to score and prioritize cyberthreats for human investigation. Some companies identify thousands of threats a day, but don't have the human resources to investigate them all. And pervasive computers across organizations generate too much data for humans to deal with on their own—an ideal situation for machine learning applications.

At Cadence Design Systems, for example, an engineering services and software company:

Between 250 and 500 gigabits of security-related data flows in daily from more than 30,000 endpoint devices and 8,200 users—and there are only 15 security analysts to look at it. "That's only some of the network data that we're getting," says Sreeni Kancharla, the company's CISO. "We actually have more. You need to have machine learning and AI so you can narrow in on the real issues and mitigate them."[29]

One downside of AI-driven cybersecurity, however, is that it generates a lot of "false positive" alarms that humans have to investigate. As Heather Adkins, head of cybersecurity at Google, pointed out at a 2017 conference:

AI is fantastic for spotting anomalous behavior, but it throws up so many false positives that knowing which is false and which is real can still only be decided by a human. For instance, if somebody has forgotten their password and tries 20 different variants, is that somebody who simply can't remember their password or a hacker trying to guess a password? This is something that an AI system would find almost impossible to work out at the moment.[30]

Not surprisingly, the leading firms in developing AI-driven approaches to cybersecurity are technology firms. One company I advise, Recorded Future, uses machine learning to identify and interpret "threat intelligence" from the internet and other data sources. Among larger firms, Apple has developed and is using a machine learning–driven approach to data privacy called "differential privacy." The company has developed several new algorithms that determine the optimal approach to privacy under a variety of circumstances.[31] Google has long employed an automated scanning system called Bouncer that scans Android apps for possibly malicious code.[32]

To sum up what nontech enterprises can do in this regard, they need to make sure that their cybersecurity professionals are aware of what is possible with AI. They should encourage cybersecurity teams to explore AI-based tools and services to leverage human efforts. However, they should not assume that human cybersecurity professionals will be replaced by cognitive technologies anytime soon.

Trust and Disclosure in AI

The sad fact is that many people don't trust decisions, answers, or recommendations from artificial intelligence. I have already cited data,
for example, that the majority of people in the United States don't
trust autonomous vehicles to drive them, even though we know that
humans don't do a great job of driving safely. Another survey of German
consumers found that just 26 percent said they would ride in an autonomous vehicle, and only 18 percent said they wanted to own one.[33]
One contributor to the trust problem is perhaps the issue of algorithmic
bias, which is becoming widely known and discussed.[34]

A variety of surveys also suggest that we humans don't trust AI across
a variety of contexts. In one survey of U.S. consumers, when presented
with a list of popular AI services (e.g., home assistants, financial planning, medical diagnosis, and hiring), 41.5 percent of respondents said
they didn't trust any of these services. Only 9 percent of respondents
said they trusted AI with their financials, and only 4 percent trusted AI in
the employee hiring process.[35] In another survey, 2,000 U.S. consumers
were asked "When you think about AI, which feelings best describe your
emotions?" "Interested" was the most common response (45 percent),
but it was closely followed by "concerned" (40.5 percent), "skeptical"
40.1 percent), "unsure" (39.1 percent), and "suspicious" (29.8 percent).
There were other, more positive responses, but they all had lower percentages of mention.[36]

What's the problem that these surveys reveal? And can it be overcome? I believe there are several different attributes of AI thus far, each
of which needs to be addressed if AI is to be trusted in businesses and
in societies.

Don't Overpromise

There is a massive amount of hype about AI, and the actual results the
technology produces will have difficulty stacking up to the hype. The
IT research firm Gartner suggests that technologies like cognitive computing, machine learning, deep learning, and cognitive expert advisors

are at the peak of their "hype cycle" and are headed toward the "trough of disillusionment."[37]

Vendor and media hype may largely be to blame for this issue. I mentioned IBM in this regard in chapter 1, which has been a problem both for its very large Watson advertising budget and its extravagant claims about Watson's abilities. One prominent AI researcher, Oren Etzioni, has called Watson "the Donald Trump of the AI industry—[making] outlandish claims that aren't backed by credible data."[38] Other vendors have also contributed to the problem, and the media has jumped on the AI bandwagon as well.

Tesla's Elon Musk is another frequent contributor to AI hype, particularly about the ability of Tesla cars to drive autonomously. The company uses the term Autopilot to describe its capabilities, which suggests full autonomy and has generated some controversy.[39] Tesla cars have some impressive semiautonomous driving capabilities and are impressive vehicles in many other respects, but they are clearly not yet fully autonomous—although Musk frequently makes claims about autonomy.

There are also examples of good practice in not overselling AI's capabilities. I mentioned the Nordic bank SEB and its use of an intelligent agent (which it calls Aida and is derived from Ipsoft's Amelia) in chapter 3. SEB has consistently been conservative in its portrayals of what Aida can do, launching it first for internal use on the IT help desk (where it is still used and is popular with employees), and then making it available to customers on an experimental basis. Aida is classified as a "trainee in the Telephone Bank." A press release from SEB captures the conservative tone, at least relative to how many describe AI systems:

At present Aida has two main duties: she has been employed as a digital employee in the bank's internal IT Service Desk, where she speaks her original language of English, and she is a trainee at the Telephone Bank, where she is learning to chat with customers in Swedish, on seb.se.... "We try to think of Aida as a person," continues Erica [Lundin, head of the Aida Center of Excellence]. "So we are building up her CV to show what she has accomplished and is competent in, and going forward we will work on her PDD [personal development dialogue] to develop her areas of competence."[40]

Whether the use of cognitive technologies is internal or external, it's best to underpromise and overdeliver. Introduce new capabilities as "beta" offerings and communicate the goal of learning about the use of the technology. Don't eliminate alternative (usually human) approaches to solving employees' or customers' problems. Over time, as the technology matures and the AI solution improves its capabilities, both the machine and the communications describing its functions can become more confident.

Disclosure

Another way to increase trust in AI systems and applications is to fully disclose as much as possible about the system and how it will be used. Disclosure might include, for example, notice that the customer is working with an "intelligent agent computer system" rather than a human representative. Or if the solution for customers and employees is a hybrid/augmented one with some human and some computerized advice, disclosure should address who does what.

Such disclosures should be crafted not by lawyers—who might wrap them up in legalese—but perhaps by marketers. The idea to get across is that this is an opportunity to try out something new, that the help is available 24/7, and that it may well address the customer's issue.

But companies need to be careful with AI in marketing. In a U.S. survey of 2000 consumers, 87 percent of respondents said they would support a rule that would prohibit AI systems such as bots, chatbots, and virtual assistants from posing as humans. More broadly, 88 percent of the respondents said that AI in marketing should be regulated by an ethical code of conduct. On the more positive side, two thirds of the surveyed Americans were open to businesses and brands using AI to communicate with them and serve them. But as the ad agency that conducted the survey notes, "The prerequisite appears to be transparency and disclosure."[41]

Certification of Models and Algorithms

As we come to rely more heavily in our society and economy on AI and machine learning, it seems likely that there will need to be some form of external certification if we are to trust the underlying models and algorithms. Just as the FDA certifies drug efficacy, auditors certify financial processes, and the Underwriters Laboratory certifies the safety of products, there will need to be trusted organizations—governmental or private sector—who endorse the reliability, replicability, and accuracy of AI algorithms.

Adam Schneider, a consultant who works in financial services, was the first to point out the possibilities of AI certification to me. He provides several examples of settings in which certification should perhaps be required:

- AI driving cars. Do we need an automated vehicle review board to understand car failures, enable comparison of different AI approaches, enable comparisons across manufacturers, and monitor progress?
- AI diagnosing patients. Do we need a protocol where human doctors verify enough of the diagnoses personally, using statistically valid techniques, before there is general reliance?
- AI "robo" investing. One firm advertised "We Have AI" that they have "Extensively Tested." Is that level of disclosure good enough? What does "We Have AI" mean? Should standards be defined before it can be advertised to unsophisticated investors?[42]

It's early for such certification to emerge, but I have heard of one actual example that is consistent with one of Schneider's examples. I interviewed a Deloitte consultant, Christopher Stevens, about his work with "robo-advisors" in investing and wealth management advice. He said that the firm was already supplying certification and advising services to financial institutions with robo-advice capabilities. It provides such services as establishment of controls and periodic effectiveness testing, evaluation of client communications and disclosures, algorithm assessment, and evaluation of compliance with trading rules.[43] I don't know whether such services will catch on in this and other marketplace domains, or whether customers will gravitate toward such certifications, but given the importance of these tests to effective use of AI, I suspect certifications will be important. It may require a highly publicized failure, however, to make certification a legal requirement.

There will probably also be more automated approaches to certifying the accuracy of AI models. UC Berkeley professor Ben Recht has commented (referring to a complex aircraft control model from Airbus):

We're trying to put (machine learning systems) in self-driving cars, power networks....If we want machine learning models to actually have an impact in everyday experience, we'd better come out with the same guarantees as one of these complicated airplane designs.[44]

The types of "guarantees" to which Recht is referring involve automated tools that would certify that a machine learning model and process would work in a production context, and also would generate a likelihood of error for them. Recht's lab at Berkeley is working on such tools, but they aren't yet ready for broad commercial implementation.

Lost Human Knowledge and Skills

A final issue relative to the impact of AI on entire societies is that of lost human ability to perform certain types of tasks. From navigation to driving to personalizing customer communications, AI is taking over substantial tasks that once required human skills and knowledge. Will humans then lose the ability to perform them?

This debate is not new, of course, and goes back to slide rules and calculators. Did they lead to humans being unable to perform long division? Not yet, anyway. And it seems likely that there would be enough humans around should the slide rules and calculators (and even more, our computers and smartphones) go away to teach us what we need to know about manual calculation methods.

I believe there are two areas in which this lost knowledge and skills discussion has merit, however. One is where we still need the knowledge and skills on a fairly regular basis. That seems likely, for example, for the foreseeable future in the area of autonomous vehicles. They now—and will probably continue to for several years—require humans to pay attention and occasionally take over. If humans aren't paying close attention, they may not be able to take over in time.

This *vigilance decrement* issue, as researchers sometimes describe it, is one of the most important factors in the design of autonomous vehicles. Firms like Alphabet's Waymo have decided that it is so important that autonomous vehicles should have no steering wheel or brakes at all. Since our society doesn't know much about this issue, several MIT researchers have begun a project to study the phenomenon of "semi-autonomous driving" to learn how humans act with regard to these capabilities.[45]

The other domain in which lost knowledge and skills are relevant is when the automation of the relevant task may permanently diminish human capabilities that would affect safety. Perhaps the most widespread concern is with commercial airline pilots, whose jets already largely steer themselves for most of the flight. Nick Carr in *The Glass Cage*[46] and others have suggested that this heavy reliance on autopilot is diminishing pilots' abilities to fly. In a less critical context, Carr and others also speculate that if people use a GPS to navigate somewhere, they don't learn much about directions in the areas in which they are using it.[47]

However, these concerns have not yet resulted in actual danger to humans. Carr admits that commercial aircraft are safer than ever to fly. Directionally clueless GPS users still get to their destinations. We should note these issues and file them under "Things We May Need to Address Seriously Someday." Beyond having pilots take the stick every once in a while in order to refresh their skills, it's not clear that further action is necessary.

Company Change Management Strategies

Thus far in this chapter I have focused on how to create trust in AI, particularly from the standpoint of customers and consumers. But trust in the technology and its implications is equally important among employees of companies that are implementing AI. The process by which that trust—and other positive social and cultural responses—is created within companies can be summarized as "change management." It is needed for any new technology, but there are some specific issues that arise when that technology is artificial intelligence.

Projects employing cognitive technology are not just about technical change, but also about changes in organizational culture, processes, behavior, and attitudes. And since they often involve the management or application of knowledge, they may be threatening to powerful and autonomous knowledge workers. If the doctors in a hospital don't trust or like using the new AI-based diagnosis system, for example, it's unlikely that the system will be successful.

Participation in the process of implementing a cognitive system is a critical factor in its success. As I've mentioned, since the technology will mean that work tasks and processes need to be redesigned, there should be an explicit design or redesign effort. And it will be much more successful if those who do the work today (or at least representatives of them) are involved in the process. Those who are closely involved can become evangelists for the new ways of working that AI makes possible. If they're not involved, they may spread negative rumors and dissatisfaction.

One example of such a participative approach in a call center is described in an IBM Watson change management guide:

> In creating a team to teach Watson, a large Telco company decided to select highly experienced call center agents and their team managers, who were dedicated to solving customer problems related to interactive TV. They collected all the questions over the last 12 months by analyzing their contact center logs. In calibration sessions, they evaluated and fine-tuned the answers based on available technical corpus as well as the logs and paired them with the questions. Another team was asked to test the solution. By investing much time and effort in teaching Watson, they came up with a valuable solution.[48]

An Augmentation Approach Helps a Lot

Cognitive technologies are particularly susceptible to fears about automation and job loss. Smart managers can dispel these early by telling workers—at least those whom they will need to keep for a while—that they won't lose their jobs because of AI. Having now seen a number of companies implement cognitive technologies, I feel even more strongly that augmentation, rather than large-scale automation, is the way to go whenever possible. If that is a firm's overall philosophy for what to do with smart machines, it helps considerably with the process of change management.

Taking an augmentation focus has many potential benefits. They include:

- Engaging your employees in figuring out how they can collaborate with smart machines
- Giving workers the security to experiment with cognitive technologies
- Creating solutions for companies and their customers that harness the best capabilities of humans and machines
- Putting the focus on productivity and growth rather than on job loss

The changes to organizations that successful AI applications require go well beyond their technical capabilities. Even if a new system works as advertised, there are many ways that humans can limit its potential. And many times the technology will have problems and quirks. So persuading human workers to embrace smart machines as colleagues with admitted flaws but high potential will greatly ease the process of adoption.

The great majority of cognitive projects I have examined (particularly in a database of over 150 consulting and advisory projects at Deloitte) have not led to substantial layoffs, and a strong majority of executives who participate in surveys say that automation-driven layoffs are not their objective. Therefore, firms might as well gain the benefits of employee engagement, loyalty, and participation by emphasizing an augmentation philosophy. They could say, for example, that jobs lost to attrition may not be replaced, but a job will remain available to any employee who is willing to stay and learn new skills. There are many ways to produce returns on investments in cognitive technologies without eliminating large numbers of jobs.

However, I recognize that AI may lead to pressures to cut costs. As one insurance executive told me recently:

We like the idea of augmentation in general. But our costs are already high relative to competitors, and we will need as much productivity as possible from these technologies. If other firms in our industry adopt AI broadly and cut jobs, we will be forced to do so as well to maintain parity with them.

The best approach to avoid this situation is to start early in redesigning business processes around AI, retraining workers, and keeping a constant focus on costs and employee performance. While retraining, it may also help from a change management perspective to formulate objective performance criteria for AI-related jobs, and to allow employees to test into (or out of) them. Then at least employees will have a fair shot at getting redesigned jobs.

Since it usually takes several years to fully implement substantial AI projects, these foci may allow a company to reshape itself to a competitive size and productivity level through attrition, or by not hiring to meet needs from growth. Achieving high productivity and lower costs through AI is not going to be easy for any competitor, and it is unlikely to happen quickly. It is almost certainly not going to happen just by installing some cognitive technologies alone.

When and for Whom Is Change Management Most Critical?

Change management related to AI doesn't hit all people equally, and there is a particular time in which it is most relevant. The time, as you might suspect, is when a pilot or proof of concept has been shown to work on a small scale, and planning begins for a full-fledged implementation. Not that there aren't some change management issues during pilots, but such projects tend to be relatively small and focused on only a few workers.

Production implementations, on the other hand, typically involve a large number of front-line workers who may not understand the technology being implemented and may even fear it. As a part of planning for full implementation, companies should develop approaches to educating and retraining workers and redesigning jobs to accommodate the capabilities of smart machines.

At least three specific types of employees are critical to the success of change management efforts. They include:

• *Experts*—Experts have a lot to gain and to lose in cognitive technology projects. They can gain in that their expertise will be captured and spread across the organization, and they may not have to answer the same boring questions over and over. They may be threatened, however, by the potential loss of exclusive or distinctive expertise, and may even fear for their jobs once the smart machine is up and running. Depending on the technology, experts may be needed to train the system before implementation. Since a lot of the expertise may be in their heads, their buy-in is necessary to extract it. After implementation, experts may also need to add cognitive system oversight and maintenance to a long list of existing responsibilities. In any case, their employers should try to keep them happy, because they will be needed to monitor and improve the system over time.

• *Decision makers*—Similar to the expert, decision makers need to be engaged in many cognitive projects. Since the goal of cognitive projects is often to improve decision making, decision makers will need to be consulted on how they currently make decisions, how they frame their decisions, and what the key variables or decision rules are in current decision-making approaches. If the goal of the project is to produce analytical insights or recommendations for a human decider, it's important to ensure that the model will actually get used (many don't). If the goal is to automate the decision to some degree, decision makers may feel threatened by cognitive projects and may impose obstacles to their success. So it's important to decide early how the system will ultimately be used and ensure that the decision maker is on board with the idea.

• *Recalcitrant learners*—At least in organizations with a commitment to augmentation, anyone willing to learn new skills and to become familiar with how smart machines work is likely to work out well in augmented roles. It is the people who are unwilling to or uninterested in learning new skills that pose a problem for augmentation approaches. They should be coaxed to learn if possible, but may ultimately need to be told that future employment depends upon their learning new skills.

The Usual Methods for Cognitive Change Management

In addition to focusing on these types of roles in production planning timeframes, all of the usual approaches to change management, including stakeholder analysis, readiness assessments, extensive communications, and coaching and training, would all seem to be relevant. Using "agile" methods for developing cognitive projects, which many companies are already doing, usually helps engage participants during the development process. While none of these change management principles is rocket science, they often seem to be overlooked.

Learning from Countries and Companies

Countries do have important influences on AI's role in society and business, for both good and bad. On the positive side, a recent article in the *New York Times* described the unconcerned attitudes of Swedish workers about AI.[49] It described an employee of a Swedish mining company who already uses remote controls to direct underground mining equipment. He believes that technological progress will eventually automate his job:

I'm not really worried.... There are so many jobs in this mine that even if this job disappears, they will have another one. The company will take care of us.

Perhaps the worker is whistling past the graveyard, but the article suggests otherwise. It describes a country in which workers are relatively calm about automation-driven job loss for several valid reasons. Government support of workers is high in Sweden. Unions are still powerful, and encourage adoption of new technologies. Trust between employers and employees is high. And when companies make more money through increased productivity they tend to share it with their workers.

The situation and worker perspective at another Sweden-based organization is similar. I've mentioned the Aida "intelligent agent" at the SEB bank a couple of times. Erica Lundin, who heads SEB's Aida Center of Excellence, says there is little concern from customer or IT service employees about job loss from Aida:

From the beginning there was not a worry about losing jobs. All of our employees were willing to help out in training Aida. They saw it as an exploration journey—applying a new technique and helping the bank figure out what can we do with it. It was never viewed as a cost saving program leading to job losses. We haven't reached the level where Aida could take over a lot of jobs anyway. That could happen in the future but it probably wouldn't involve getting rid of people.

This reassuring national context for job security may not prevail in your country, and it doesn't in mine. But that doesn't mean that individual companies outside of Scandinavia can't try to create similar environments. The upside for them would be high levels of employee loyalty, collaboration, and willingness to adopt new technologies. And as MIT researcher Zeynep Ton has demonstrated—particularly in the retail industry, but in others as well—this "good jobs strategy" (whether or not it involves AI or other new technologies) can also yield high levels of financial performance for the companies that adopt it.[50] As Ton and a colleague of hers describe the strategy:

The Good Jobs Strategy enables companies to make the most of their employees' full potential. So good jobs companies are less likely to focus on machines replacing workers and more likely to focus on machines as a valuable complement to their valuable people. When one of us visited Mercadona's [a Spanish retailer described as following the Good Jobs Strategy] fully automated distribution center, the director said, "Its construction was based on one premise: Don't make a person do what a machine can do. The only effort we want from our employees is for them to give us their skills and their knowledge."[51]

Sweden and Mercadona are completely different types of entities, but they have taken similar approaches to integrating AI and automation into their workforces. They're also both highly successful in economic terms. Other companies and organizations can adopt similar approaches and reap similar benefits.

Summary and Conclusions

This chapter is perhaps the most speculative of all in a book that—given its topic—can't totally avoid speculation. While many enterprises are now implementing cognitive technologies, many have not yet gotten to the stage in which change management issues become paramount. The chapter also raises issues that may not have occurred yet to those responsible for making AI a reality, but it is likely that they will pop up to some degree in many organizations.

It's important to remember as well that many organizations have faced somewhat similar change management issues with previous generations of information technologies. New technologies almost always lead to some change in how work is done if they are to provide some value. New work processes from new technology have almost always benefitted from redesign efforts involving those who do the work. And even the threat of automation-driven job loss has been present with previous technologies—though perhaps not to the same degree as with AI.

Just as in the past, we'll have to learn about these technologies as they mature and are implemented more broadly. Just as with previous generations of technology, we will need to achieve some economic and productivity benefits if they are to provide value to businesses. And just as in the past, firms will need to balance the opportunities from automating and making processes smarter with the impact on the people in their organizations and their jobs.

All we know for sure is that people won't do all the work in the future, and machines won't either. The details of how humans and machines collaborate to accomplish key tasks will have to be discovered, negotiated, and revisited on a case-by-case basis. Firms and their managers should keep the primary goal in mind of establishing productive, effective, and humane AI solutions over time.

This last somewhat ambiguous message—we're not sure how things will work out with humans and AI and some combination of automation and augmentation is likely to result—is perhaps true of the whole field and this entire book. On the one hand, I've claimed throughout that AI/cognitive technologies are potentially transformative of business strategies and processes, and that every company should be moving forward with them. On the other hand, I urge some degree of caution—picking the low hanging fruit over the dramatic, transformational moon shots that are a good bet to fail given today's technologies. I've also argued that it's getting easier and cheaper to create AI models and algorithms, but that the hard part of the technology is integrating it with existing systems and processes, and changing individual behaviors and organizational cultures.

I think we'll be living with these nuances for a while. And in a sense they are no different than adoption approaches for other types of technologies. In addition to embracing AI, many companies today are trying to achieve digital transformation in general. But some of the established companies that embraced digital transformation most aggressively—GE, Nike, Procter & Gamble, and Burberry, for example—have been forced to retrench and prioritize the expensive investments needed to digitize every process.

We also saw these tensions with the last technology that reshaped business—the internet and electronic commerce. There was undoubtedly a lot of power in the technology, and we came to realize that it would disrupt industries and reshape business strategies and models. Established companies justifiably felt plenty of pressure from startups that did or could enter their industries with digitally centric business models. Yet it turned out that the unquestioning embrace of websites, e-commerce, and online business was no savior for startups with eyeballs rather than revenues, or for e-commerce business models that didn't appeal to customers.

Artificial intelligence holds fantastic promise for extending the reach and range of human capabilities. A company with no AI capabilities is as foolish as a company with no internet presence, or one that insists on using only analog, paper-based business processes. Just as the late 1990s and early 2000s heralded the age of the internet, the time for AI in the enterprise is here. If your company's direct competitors aren't already embracing it, disruptive startups will. Of course, that doesn't mean that good business judgment about the adoption and use of artificial intelligence won't be just as important as it was for previous technologies. Employing that judgment and learning through experimentation and experience will mean that companies can benefit enormously from some of the most exciting and powerful technologies ever created by human beings.

Notes

Chapter 1

1. Memorial Sloan Kettering press release, "Memorial Sloan Kettering Cancer Center and IBM Will Collaborate on Powerful New Medical Technology," June 5, 2012, https://www.mskcc.org/blog/mskcc-and-ibm-will-collaborate-powerful-new-medical-technology

2. Laura Nathan-Garner, "The Future of Cancer Treatment and Research: What IBM Watson Means for Our Patients," M.D. Anderson Cancerwise blog, November 12, 2013, https://www.mdanderson.org/publications/cancerwise/2013/11/what-ibm-watson-means-for-our-patients.html

3. Spencer E. Ante, "IBM Struggles to Turn Watson Computer into Big Business," *Wall Street Journal*, January 7, 2014, https://www.wsj.com/articles/ibm-struggles-to-turn-watson-computer-into-big-business-1389142136

4. Ariana Eunjung Cha, "IBM Supercomputer Watson's Next Feat? Taking on Cancer," *Washington Post*, June 27, 2015, http://www.washingtonpost.com/sf/national/2015/06/27/watsons-next-feat-taking-on-cancer/

5. "Research Platform for the Moon Shots Program—APOLLO," M.D. Anderson Cancer Center website, accessed February 12, 2018, https://www.mdanderson.org/cancermoonshots/research_platforms/apollo.html

6. "Machine Learning at AWS" website, accessed February 11, 2018, https://aws.amazon.com/machine-learning/

7. Glassdoor, Amazon.com "data scientist" openings, accessed February 11, 2018.

8. "Bezos Letter to Shareholders," CNBC, https://www.cnbc.com/2017/04/12/amazon-jeff-bezos-2017-shareholder-letter.html

9. Susan Ratcliffe, ed., "Roy Amara 1925–2007, American Futurologist," *Oxford Essential Quotations* (4th ed.) (Oxford University Press, 2016).

10. Kevin Kelly, "The Three Breakthroughs That Have Finally Unleashed AI on the World," *Wired*, October 27, 2014, https://www.wired.com/2014/10/future-of-artificial-intelligence/

11. Daniel Schreiber, "AI Eats Insurance," Lemonade blog post, January 8, 2018, https://www.lemonade.com/blog/ai-eats-insurance/

12. Kris Hammond, "A Periodic Table of AI," AI XPrize website, December 14, 2016, https://ai.xprize.org/news/periodic-table-of-ai

13. James Somers, "Is AI Riding a One-Trick Pony?," *MIT Technology Review*, September 29, 2017, https://www.technologyreview.com/s/608911/is-ai-riding-a-one-trick-pony/

14. Mathew Mayo, "The Current State of Automated Machine Learning," KDNuggets blog post, January 25, 2017, https://www.kdnuggets.com/2017/01/current-state-automated-machine-learning.html

15. Alex Irpan, "Deep Reinforcement Learning Doesn't Work Yet," Sorta Insightful blog post, February 14, 2018, https://www.alexirpan.com/2018/02/14/rl-hard.html

16. Doug Williams, "How Is RPA Different from Other Enteprise Automation Tools Such as BPM/ODM," IBM Consulting Blog, July 10, 2017, https://www.ibm.com/blogs/insights-on-business/gbs-strategy/rpa-different-enterprise-automation-tools-bpmodm/

17. Steven Norton, "The Morning Download," *Wall Street Journal* CIO Journal, December 29, 2017, https://blogs.wsj.com/cio/2017/12/29/cios-aim-to-make-ai-useful-hire-the-right-people-to-manage-it-in-2018/

18. Jack Clark, "Why 2015 Was a Breakthrough Year in Artificial Intelligence," Bloomberg.

19. Sapna Maheshwari and Mike Isaac, "Facebook, After 'Fail' over Ads Targeting Racists, Makes Changes," *New York Times*, September 21, 2017, https://www.nytimes.com/2017/09/20/business/media/facebook-racist-ads.html

20. Tom Simonte, "Humans Can't Expect AI to Just Fight Fake News for Them," *WIRED*, June 15, 2017, https://www.wired.com/story/fake-news-challenge-artificial-intelligence/

21. Barb Darrow, "Has IBM's AI Technology Fallen Victim to Hype?," *Fortune*, June 28, 2017, http://fortune.com/2017/06/28/ibm-watson-ai-healthcare/

22. Casey Ross and Ike Swetlitz, "IBM Pitched Watson as a Revolution in Cancer Care. It's Nowhere Close," STAT website, September 5, 2017, https://www.statnews.com/2017/09/05/watson-ibm-cancer/

23. James Kisner et al., "Creating Shareholder Value with AI? Not So Elementary, My Dear Watson," Jefferies Research Report, July 12, 2017, available at: https://javatar.bluematrix.com/pdf/fO5xcWjc

Chapter 2

1. Jacques Bughin et al., "Artificial Intelligence: The Next Digital Frontier?" McKinsey Global Institute, June 2017, https://www.mckinsey.com/business-functions/mckinsey-analytics/our-insights/how-artificial-intelligence-can-deliver-real-value-to-companies

2. Whitney L. Jackson, "Imaging Utilization Trends and Reimbursement," Diagnostic Imaging website, July 21, 2014, http://www.diagnosticimaging.com/reimbursement/imaging-utilization-trends-and-reimbursement

3. Cisco information from interviews with company executives and Alex Woodie, "Inside Cisco's Machine Learning Model Factory," Datanami website, January 12, 2015, https://www.datanami.com/2015/01/12/inside-ciscos-machine-learning-model-factory/

4. Information about Macy's from interviews with company executives and "Macy's Uses AI-Driven Virtual Agent to Transform Online and Mobile Customer Service," Microsoft website, September 25, 2017, https://customers.microsoft.com/en-us/story/macys-retail-microsoft-ai

5. Gill Pratt, "Is a Cambrian Explosion Coming for Robotics?" *Journal of Economic Perspectives* 29 (3) (2015): 51–60, https://www.aeaweb.org/articles?id=10.1257/jep.29.3.51

6. Cade Metz, "Tech Giants Are Paying Huge Salaries for Scarce AI Talent," *New York Times*, October 22, 2017, https://www.nytimes.com/2017/10/22/technology/artificial-intelligence-experts-salaries.html

7. Steven Norton, "The Morning Download," *Wall Street Journal* CIO Journal, December 29, 2017, https://blogs.wsj.com/cio/2017/12/29/cios-aim-to-make-ai-useful-hire-the-right-people-to-manage-it-in-2018/

8. Laurence Goasduff, "2018 Will Mark the Beginning of AI Democratization," Gartner Inc. website, December 19, 2017, https://www.gartner.com/smarterwithgartner/2018-will-mark-the-beginning-of-ai-democratization/

9. Seth Earley, "There Is No AI without IA," *IT Professional* 18 (May–June 2016): 58–64, doi:10.1109/MITP.2016.43

Chapter 3

1. This chapter is a revised and expanded version of the article by Thomas H. Davenport and Rajeev Ronanki, "Artificial Intelligence for the Real World," *Harvard Business Review*, January–February 2018.

2. "Burning Passion to Use AI for World-Class Service," SEBGroup press release, August 21, 2017, https://sebgroup.com/press/news/burning-passion-to-use-ai-for -world-class-service; the use of Amelia at SEB is also described in a case study by Mary Lacity, Leslie Willcocks, and Andrew Craig, "Service Automation: Cognitive Virtual Agents at SEB Bank," London School of Economics Outsourcing Unit Working Research Paper Series, February 2017, http://www.umsl.edu/~lacitym /LSEOUWP1701.pdf

3. Shareen Pathak, "Drop It Like It's Bot: Brands Have Cooled on Chatbots," Digiday, March 10, 2017, https://digiday.com/marketing/brand-bot-backlash -begun/

4. "Consumers Say No to Chatbot Silos in US and UK Survey," eGain press release, February 7, 2018, http://www.egain.com/company/news/press_releases /consumers-say-no-chatbot-silos-us-uk-survey/

5. "Nvidia Partner Jetson Stories: Fellow Robots—LoweBot—Lowe's Innova- tion Labs," March 30, 2017, http://www.lowesinnovationlabs.com/updates /2017/3/30/nvidia-jetson-partner-stories-fellow-robots-lowebot

Chapter 4

1. Thanks to Vikram Mahidhar, who leads the AI business at Genpact, for help- ing me with many of the ideas in this chapter, particularly with regard to the key decisions that companies need to make in their strategies.

2. Frederic Lardinois, "Big Data Platform Databricks Raises $140M Series D Round Led by Andreesen Horowitz," TechCrunch website, August 22, 2017, https://techcrunch.com/2017/08/22/big-data-analytics-platform-databricks -raises-140m-series-d-round-led-by-andreessen-horowitz/

3. "Bullish on the Business Value of Cognitive," Deloitte LLC, November 2017, https://www2.deloitte.com/content/dam/Deloitte/us/Documents/deloitte -analytics/us-da-2017-deloitte-state-of-cognitive-survey.pdf

4. Genpact and Fortune Knowledge Group, "Is Your Business AI-Ready?" September 18, 2017, https://fortunefkg.com/wp-content/uploads/2017/09/Genpact -white-paper.cm_.9.18.17.WEB-FINAL.pdf

5. Teradata, "State of Artificial Intelligence for Enterprises," 2017, http://assets .teradata.com/resourceCenter/downloads/ExecutiveBriefs/EB9867_State_of _Artificial_Intelligence_for_the_Enterprises.pdf

6. "Gartner Says AI Technologies Will Be in Almost Every New Software Product by 2020," Gartner Inc. press release, July 18, 2017, https://www.gartner.com /newsroom/id/3763265

7. Jacques Bughin et al., "Artificial Intelligence: The Next Digital Frontier?" McKinsey Global Institute, June 2017, https://www.mckinsey.com/business -functions/mckinsey-analytics/our-insights/how-artificial-intelligence-can -deliver-real-value-to-companies

8. Satya Ramaswamy, "How Companies Are Already Using AI," *Harvard Business Review,* April 14, 2017, https://hbr.org/2017/04/how-companies-are-already -using-ai

9. Information about GE customer data from company executives and John Moore, "GE Digital Thread Now Runs through a 'Hub' Customer Database," TechTarget, September 2017, http://searchcio.techtarget.com/feature/GE-digital -thread-now-runs-through-a-hub-customer-database

10. Mariya Yao, "Capital One Seals Tech Street Cred with Forays into AI," Topbots website post, April 7, 2017, https://www.topbots.com/capital-one-seals -tech-street-cred-forays-ai/

11. Bonnie McGeer, "Capital One Shortens the Machine Learning Curve," American Banker website, April 26, 2017, https://www.americanbanker.com /opinion/capital-one-shortens-the-machine-learning-curve

12. Will Knight, "The Financial World Wants to Open AI's Black Boxes," *MIT Technology Review,* April 13, 2017, https://www.technologyreview.com/s/604122 /the-financial-world-wants-to-open-ais-black-boxes/

13. See, for example, Barry Libert, Megan Beck, and Yoram Wind, *The Network Imperative* (Harvard Business Review Press, 2016).

14. Martin Reeves et al., "The Truth About Corporate Transformation," *MIT Sloan Management Review,* January 31, 2018, https://sloanreview.mit.edu/article /the-truth-about-corporate-transformation/

15. Gary Marcus and Ernest Davis, "Do We Really Need to Learn to Code?" *New Yorker*, June 6, 2014, https://www.newyorker.com/tech/elements/do-we-really -need-to-learn-to-code

16. Pete Singer, "Enabling the AI Era," Semiconductor Manufacturing and Design Community website, October 23, 2017, http://semimd.com/blog/2017 /10/23/enabling-the-a-i-era/

17. Jeff Walsh, "Machine Learning: The Speed-of-Light Evolution of AI and Design," Redshift by Autodesk online newsletter, May 5, 2016, https://www .autodesk.com/redshift/machine-learning/

18. Dimitar Mihov, "Airbnb Built an AI That Turns Design Sketches into Source Code, " The Next Web website, October 26, 2017, https://thenextweb.com /artificial-intelligence/2017/10/25/airbnb-ai-sketches-design-code/

19. Geoffrey Ling and Blake Bextine, "Precision Agriculture Increases Crop Yields," *Scientific American*, June 26, 2016, https://www.scientificamerican.com /article/precision-farming/

20. Van Noorden R., "Scientists May Be Reaching a Peak in Reading Habits," http://ibm.biz/BdrAjS, February 3, 2014.

21. "Table of Experts: Technology Trends and the Skills Needed to Lead," *St. Louis Business Journal*, April 14, 2017, https://www.bizjournals.com/stlouis /news/2017/04/14/table-of-experts-technology-trends-and-the-skills.html

22. Steve Rosenbush, "The Morning Download: CIO Compensation Rises 37% in Two Years," Wall Street Journal CIO Journal website, October 27, 2017, https://blogs.wsj.com/cio/2017/10/27/the-morning-download-cio-compen sation-rises-37-in-two-years/

23. Kevin Roose, "Can Ford Become a Tech Company?" *New York Times*, November 12, 2017, https://www.nytimes.com/interactive/2017/11/09/maga zine/tech-design-autonomous-future-cars-detroit-ford.html

24. Dana Hull, "Toyota Turns to AI for a Better Electric Car," Bloomberg Markets website, March 30, 2017, https://www.bloomberg.com/news/articles/2017 -03-30/toyota-lets-ai-loose-on-hunt-for-fuel-cell-battery-breakthrough

25. Blair Hanley Frank, "Lyft to Open-Source Some of Its AI Algorithm Testing Tools," VentureBeat website, July 12, 2017, https://venturebeat.com/2017/07 /12/lyft-to-open-source-some-of-its-ai-algorithm-testing-tools/

26. Jeremy Hermann and Mike Del Balso, "Meet Michelangelo: Uber's Machine Learning Platform," Uber Engineering website blogpost, September 5, 2017, https://eng.uber.com/michelangelo/

27. Chintan Turakhia, "Engineering More Reliable Transportation with ML and AI at Uber," Uber Engineering website blogpost, November 10, 2017, https:// eng.uber.com/machine-learning/

28. Enlitic website, accessed on November 14, 2017, https://www.enlitic.com /index.html

29. Interview with Paul English, Business Travel News website, October 4, 2017, http://www.businesstravelnews.com/Interviews/Paul-English-on-Lolas-Debut -for-Business-Travelers-Today

30. Will Knight, "An AI with 30 Years' Worth of Knowledge Finally Goes to Work," *MIT Technology Review*, March 14, 2016, https://www.technologyreview .com/s/600984/an-ai-with-30-years-worth-of-knowledge-finally-goes-to-work/

31. Robert Wachter, "Will Computers Ever Be as Good as Physicians at Diagnosing Patients?" KQED The Future of You website, November 7, 2016, https:// www.kqed.org/futureofyou/2016/11/07/will-computers-ever-be-able-to-make -diagnoses-as-well-as-physicians/

32. David Trainer, "Big Banks Big Bets to Win the Fintech Revolution," Forbes blog post, October 16, 2017, https://www.forbes.com/sites/greatspeculations /2017/10/16/big-banks-big-favorites-to-win-fintech-revolution/.

33. Kimberly Teti et al., "The Different Approaches Firms Use to Set Strategy," *Harvard Business Review* online article, April 10, 2017, https://hbr.org/2017/04 /the-different-approaches-firms-use-to-set-strategy

34. Jeremy Kahn, "Just How Shallow Is the Artificial Intelligence Talent Pool?," Information Management website, February 7, 2018, https://www.information -management.com/news/just-how-shallow-is-the-artificial-intelligence-talent -pool?

35. Will Knight, "You Could Become an AI Master Before You Know It. Here's How," *MIT Technology Review*, October 17, 2017, https://www.technologyreview .com/s/608921/you-could-become-an-ai-master-before-you-know-it-heres -how/

36. "The Race for AI: Google, Baidu, Intel, Apple in a Rush to Grab Artificial Intelligence Startups," CBInsights Research Brief, July 21, 2017, https://www .cbinsights.com/research/top-acquirers-ai-startups-ma-timeline/

37. Alan Ohnsman, "GM's Cruise Poised to Add 1,100 Silicon Valley Self-Driving Car Tech Jobs," *Forbes*, April 4, 2017, https://www.forbes.com/sites/alanohns man/2017/04/04/gms-cruise-poised-to-add-1100-silicon-valley-autonomous -car-tech-jobs/

38. Andrew Brust, "Nvidia Swings for the AI Fences," ZDNet, January 11, 2018, http://www.zdnet.com/article/nvidia-swings-for-the-ai-fences/

39. Paul Mozur, "Beijing Wants A.I. to Be Made in China by 2030," *New York Times*, July 20, 2017, https://www.nytimes.com/2017/07/20/business/china-artificial-intelligence.html

40. Christina Larson, "China's Massive Investment in Artificial Intelligence Has an Insidious Downside," *Science*, February 8, 2018, http://www.sciencemag.org/news/2018/02/china-s-massive-investment-artificial-intelligence-has-insidious-downside

41. Aaron Tan, "Singapore Taps AI in Industry Transformation," Computer-Weekly website, November 3, 2017, http://www.computerweekly.com/news/450429369/Singapore-taps-AI-in-industry-transformation

42. "Budget 2017: Funding for AI, 5G and Digital Skills," BBC website, November 22, 2017, http://www.bbc.com/news/technology-42081703

43. Richard Stirling, Hannah Miller, and Emma Martinho-Trusswell, "Government AI Readiness Index," December 2017, https://www.oxfordinsights.com/government-ai-readiness-index/

44. Charlie Taylor, "Thriving AI Ecosystem Developing in Ireland, Figures Show," Irish Times website, Sept. 28, 2017, https://www.irishtimes.com/business/technology/thriving-ai-ecosystem-developing-in-ireland-figures-show-1.3235768

45. "Pan-Canadian Artificial Intelligence Strategy Overview," Canadian Institute for Advanced Research, March 30, 2017, https://www.cifar.ca/assets/pan-canadian-artificial-intelligence-strategy-overview/

46. Ajay Agarwal, Joshua Gans, and Avi Goldfarb, "The Obama Administration's Roadmap for AI Policy," Harvard Business Review website, December 21, 2016, https://hbr.org/2016/12/the-obama-administrations-roadmap-for-ai-policy

47. Amy Webb, "Trump's Treasury Secretary Is an Artificial Intelligence Denier," *Los Angeles Times*, March 28, 2017, http://www.latimes.com/opinion/op-ed/la-oe-webb-ai-mnuchin-20170328-story.html

48. Christopher Matthews, "How AI Is Taking over the Global Economy in One Chart," *Axios*, June 18, 2017, https://www.axios.com/how-ai-is-taking-over-the-global-economy-in-one-chart-1513303050-f4f4f807-5d32-4a2d-bf8c-8d639c41849d.html

Chapter 5

1. Sam Schechner, "Meet Your New Boss: An Algorithm," *Wall Street Journal*, December 10, 2017, https://www.wsj.com/articles/meet-your-new-boss-an-algori thm-1512910800

2. "Andrew Ng Shares the Astonishing Ways Deep Learning Is Changing the World," Import.io website, 2016, accessed December 14, 2017, https://www .import.io/post/andrew-ng-shares-the-astonishing-ways-deep-learning-is -changing-the-world/

3. Sten Lock, "Denmark's Largest Bank Is Using Machine Learning and AI to 'Tear Everything Apart'—and Customers Love It," *Nordic Business Insider*, November 1, 2017, http://nordic.businessinsider.com/denmarks-largest-bank -is-using-machine-learning-to-predict-the-customers-behavior--and-they-like-it -2017-11/ also Bjørn Büchmann-Slorup, Danske Bank, "Customer Retention" presentation at COMEX Implement conference, April 29, 2016, http://imple mentconsultinggroup.com/media/2635/customer_retention_comex_160429 -danske-bank-praesentation.pdf

4. Greg Nichols, "3D Vision and AI Are About to Solve the Biggest Problem in Construction, ZDNet, January 24, 2018, http://www.zdnet.com/article/3d -vision-and-ai-are-about-to-solve-the-biggest-problem-in-construction/

5. Amazon Go Frequently Asked Questions, accessed December 14, 2017, https:// www.amazon.com/b?node=16008589011

6. Zeynep Ton, *The Good Jobs Strategy* (New Harvest Press, 2014).

7. Geoffrey Smith, "Facebook Is Being Accused of Publishing Child Pornogra- phy," *Fortune*, April 13, 2017, http://fortune.com/2017/04/13/facebook-child -pornographyd-terrorist-propaganda/

8. Charlie Warzel, "Here's What YouTube Is Doing to Stop Its Child Exploita- tion Problem," Buzzfeed website, December 4, 2017, https://www.buzzfeed.com /charliewarzel/youtube-will-add-more-human-moderators-to-stop-its-child

9. Greg Lamm, "Amazon's Having Problems with Its Cashier-Free Amazon Go Test Store," *Puget Sound Business Journal*, March 27, 2017, http://fortune.com /2017/04/13/facebook-child-pornographyd-terrorist-propaganda/, and Jason Del Rey, "Amazon's Store of the Future Is Delayed. Insert 'Told Ya So' from Skeptical Retail Execs," Recode website, March 27, 2017, https://www.recode.net/2017/3 /27/15072084/amazons-go-future-store-delayed-opening

10. "Face Recognition Technology," The American Civil Liberties Union website, accessed December 4, 2017, https://www.aclu.org/issues/privacy-technology/surveillance-technologies/face-recognition-technology

11. Greg Nichols, "Robotics in Business: Everything Humans Need to Know," ZDNet website, January 11, 2018, http://www.zdnet.com/article/robotics-in-business-everything-humans-need-to-know/

12. Jonathan Vanian, "Robotics Market to Hit $135 Billion in 2019," *Fortune*, February 24, 2016, http://fortune.com/2016/02/24/robotics-market-multi-billion-boom/

13. Amanda Little, "This Army of AI Robots Will Feed the World," *Bloomberg Businessweek*, January 11, 2018, https://www.bloomberg.com/news/features/2018-01-11/this-army-of-ai-robots-will-feed-the-world

14. Daron Acemoglu and Pascual Restrepo, "Robots and Jobs: Evidence from US Labor Markets," National Bureau of Economic Research working paper, March 2017, http://www.nber.org/papers/w23285

15. Nick Wingfield, "As Amazon Pushes Forward with Robots, Workers Find New Roles," *New York Times*, September 10, 2017, https://www.nytimes.com/2017/09/10/technology/amazon-robots-workers.html

16. Rodney Brooks, "The Real Problem with Self-Driving Cars Is People," *IEEE Spectrum*, July 27, 2017, https://spectrum.ieee.org/transportation/self-driving/the-big-problem-with-selfdriving-cars-is-people

17. Brant D. McLaughlin, "Self-Driving Car Perceptions and Attitudes in the U.S.," Talking New Media website, July 27, 2017, http://www.talkingnewmedia.com/2017/07/27/self-driving-car-perceptions-attitudes-u-s/

18. Srini Pillay, "Facebook's AI for Suicide Prevention Is a Bad Idea," *Fortune*, November 30, 2017, http://fortune.com/2017/11/30/facebook-ai-suicide-prevention/

19. Several of these applications are described on the Affectiva website (accessed December 8, 2017): https://www.affectiva.com/what/uses/automotive/

20. Yuting Lu, Marwa Mahmoud, and Peter Robinson. "Estimating sheep pain level using facial action unit detection," paper presented to the IEEE International Conference on Automatic Face and Gesture Recognition, Washington, D.C., 30 May–3 June, 2017. http://www.fg2017.org/.

21. Morgan Winsor, "Facebook to Hire 3,000 More Workers to Monitor Content amid Surge of Violent Videos," ABC News website, May 3, 2017, http://

abcnews.go.com/Technology/facebook-hire-3000-workers-monitor-content/story?id=47178969

22. Maja Pantic and Leon J.M. Rothkrantz, "Automatic Analysis of Facial Expressions: The State of the Art," *IEEE Transactions on Pattern Analysis and Machine Intelligence* 22(2) (December 2000), https://repository.tudelft.nl/islandora/object/uuid:ff32a736-1535-4752-8bf2-8ae51f5c677d/datastream/OBJ

23. Thomas H. Davenport, *Process Innovation: Reengineering Work through Information Technology* (Harvard Business Review Press, 1993); Michael Hammer and James Champy, *Reengineering the Corporation* (Harper Collins 1993).

24. Robert J. Gordon, *The Rise and Fall of American Growth* (Princeton University Press, 2016).

25. Thomas H. Davenport, "The Fad That Forgot People," *Fast Company*, October 1995, https://www.fastcompany.com/26310/fad-forgot-people

26. Manoj Saxena, "What's Still Missing from the AI Revolution," *Fast Co. Design*, February 8, 2017, https://www.fastcodesign.com/3068005/whats-still-missing-from-the-ai-revolution

Chapter 6

1. Martin Ford, *Rise of the Robots* (Basic Books, 2015).

2. Jerry Kaplan, *Humans Need Not Apply: A Guide to Wealth and Work in the Age of Artificial Intelligence* (Yale University Press, 2014).

3. Karl-Benedikt Frey and Michael Osborne, "The Future of Employment: How Susceptible Are Jobs to Computerisation?" Oxford Martin Institute, 2013, https://www.oxfordmartin.ox.ac.uk/downloads/academic/The_Future_of_Employment.pdf

4. "From Brawn to Brains: The Impact of Technology on Jobs in the UK," Deloitte, 2015, https://www2.deloitte.com/content/dam/Deloitte/uk/Documents/Growth/deloitte-uk-insights-from-brawns-to-brain.pdf

5. M. Arntz, T. Gregory, and U. Zierahn, "The Risk of Automation for Jobs in OECD Countries," OECD research paper, May 2016, http://www.oecd-ilibrary.org/social-issues-migration-health/the-risk-of-automation-for-jobs-in-oecd-countries_5jlz9h56dvq7-en

6. Richard Berriman and John Hawksworth, "Will Robots Steal Our Jobs? The Potential Impact of Automation on the UK and Other Major Economies, PWC

UK Economic Outlook, March 2017, https://www.pwc.co.uk/economic-services /ukeo/pwcukeo-section-4-automation-march-2017-v2.pdf

7. Michael Chui, James Manyika, and Mehdi Miremadi, "Four Fundamentals of Workplace Automation," McKinsey Global Institute, November 2015, https://www.mckinsey.com/business-functions/digital-mckinsey/our-insights /four-fundamentals-of-workplace-automation

8. James Manyika et al., "Harnessing Automation for a Future That Works," McKinsey Global Institute, January 2017, https://www.mckinsey.com/global -themes/digital-disruption/harnessing-automation-for-a-future-that-works

9. Thomas H. Davenport and Julia Kirby, *Only Humans Need Apply: Winners and Losers in the Age of Smart Machines* (Harper Business, 2016).

10. Jacques Bughin et al., "How Artificial Intelligence Can Deliver Real Value to Companies," McKinsey Global Institute, June 2017, https://www.mckinsey.com /business-functions/mckinsey-analytics/our-insights/how-artificial-intelligence -can-deliver-real-value-to-companies

11. "Is Your Business AI-Ready?" Genpact and Fortune Knowledge Group, 2017, http://www.genpact.com/downloadable-content/insight/is-your-business-ai -ready.pdf

12. "Genpact Research Finds Few Workers Believe AI Threatens Their Jobs," Genpact press release, November 14, 2017, http://www.genpact.com/about -us/media/press-releases/2017-few-workers-believe-artificial-intelligence-ai-will -threaten-their-jobs

13. The Deloitte projects are described in Thomas H. Davenport and Rajeev Ronanki, "Artificial Intelligence for the Real World," *Harvard Business Review*, January-February 2018.

14. James Bessen, *Learning by Doing: The Real Connection between Innovation, Wages, and Wealth* (Yale University Press, 2015).

15. Dana Remus and Frank S., Levy, "Can Robots Be Lawyers? Computers, Lawyers, and the Practice of Law" (November 27, 2016). Available at SSRN: https:// ssrn.com/abstract=2701092.

16. Luke Oakden-Rayner, "The End of Human Doctors—Radiologist Escape Velocity," blog post, May 8, 2017, https://lukeoakdenrayner.wordpress.com /2017/05/08/the-end-of-human-doctors-radiology-escape-velocity/

17. Angus Loten, "AI to Drive Job Growth by 2020: Gartner," *Wall Street Journal*, December 15, 2017, https://blogs.wsj.com/cio/2017/12/15/ai-to-drive-job -growth-by-2020-gartner/

18. Cognizant Center for the Future of Work, "21 Jobs of the Future," November 28, 2017, https://www.cognizant.com/perspectives/21-jobs-of-the-future

19. Jeanne Ross, "The Fundamental Flaw in AI Implementation," *MIT Sloan Management Review*, July 14, 2017, https://sloanreview.mit.edu/article/the-fundamental-flaw-in-ai-implementation/

20. H. James Wilson, Paul Daugherty, and Nicola Morini-Bianzino, "The Jobs That Artificial Intelligence Will Create," *MIT Sloan Management Review*, https://sloanreview.mit.edu/article/will-ai-create-as-many-jobs-as-it-eliminates/

21. Paul R. Dougherty and H. James Wilson, *Human + Machine: Reimagining Work in the Age of AI* (Harvard Business Review Press, 2018).

22. Thomas H. Davenport and Julia Kirby, *Only Humans Need Apply: Winners and Losers in the Age of Smart Machines* (Harper Business, 2016).

23. "Path to Autonomy: Self-Driving Car Levels 0 to 5 Explained," *Car and Driver,* Octover 2017, https://www.caranddriver.com/features/path-to-autonomy-self-driving-car-levels-0-to-5-explained-feature

24. Anand Rao, "A Strategist's Guide to Artificial Intelligence," *Strategy + Business*, May 10, 2017, https://www.strategy-business.com/article/A-Strategists-Guide-to-Artificial-Intelligence

25. Thomas H. Davenport and Julia Kirby, "Just How Smart Are Smart Machines?" *MIT Sloan Management Review*, Spring 2016, https://sloanreview.mit.edu/article/just-how-smart-are-smart-machines/

26. Becky Peterson, "GitHub CEO Wanstrath Says Automation Will Replace Software Coding," *Business Insider*, October 11, 2017, http://www.businessinsider.com/github-ceo-wanstrath-says-automation-will-replace-software-coding-2017-10

27. Bob Kegan, panel discussion at the Consortium for Advancing Adult Learning and Development, in "Getting Ready for the Future of Work," McKinsey.com, September 2017, https://www.mckinsey.com/business-functions/organization/our-insights/getting-ready-for-the-future-of-work

28. Will Carson, "Bank of America Opens Automated Branches for Digital Banking," Corporate Insight website, http://corporateinsight.com/bank-of-america-opens-automated-branches-for-digital-banking/

29. Genpact and Fortune Knowledge Group, "Is Your Business AI-Ready?" September 18, 2017, https://fortunefkg.com/wp-content/uploads/2017/09/Genpact-white-paper.cm_.9.18.17.WEB-FINAL.pdf

Chapter 7

1. Teradata, State of Artificial Intelligence for Enterprises, Executive Summary, 2017, http://assets.teradata.com/resourceCenter/downloads/ExecutiveBriefs /EB9867_State_of_Artificial_Intelligence_for_the_Enterprises.pdf

2. Thomas H. Davenport and Julia Kirby, "Just How Smart Are Smart Machines?," *MIT Sloan Management Review*, Spring 2016, https://sloanreview.mit.edu/article /just-how-smart-are-smart-machines/

3. These company results were presented at the 2017 Dreamforce conference in November 2017, which I attended, by either the particular companies or by Salesforce.com personnel.

4. Amit Chowdhry, "How SAP Is Utilizing Machine Learning for Its Enterprise Applications," *Forbes*, January 19, 2018, https://www.forbes.com/sites /amitchowdhry/2018/01/19/how-sap-is-utilizing-machine-learning-for-its -enterprise-applications/.

5. For a description of some of these vendors' capabilities in customer relationship management, see Jon Walker, "CRM Artificial Intelligence Trends Across Salesforce, Oracle, SAP and More," Techemergence website, December 25, 2017, https://www.techemergence.com/crm-artificial-intelligence-trends-across -salesforce-oracle-sap/

6. James Kisner et al., "Creating Shareholder Value with AI? Not So Elementary, My Dear Watson," Jefferies Research Report, July 12, 2017, available at: https:// javatar.bluematrix.com/pdf/fO5xcWjc

7. Michael Stonebraker, "Traditional MDM Solutions Struggle to Master Data at Scale," Tamr White Paper, August 2017, http://www.tamr.com/wp-content /uploads/2017/08/Scalable-Data-Curation-and-Data-Mastering_082417.pdf

8. The Bank of Montreal example is drawn with modifications from Thomas H. Davenport and Randy Bean, "Setting the Table for Data Science and AI at Bank of Montreal," *Forbes*, December 8, 2017, https://www.forbes.com/sites/tomdaven port/2017/12/08/setting-the-table-for-data-science-and-ai-at-bank-of-montreal/

9. For a discussion of defense and offense-oriented applications of data and analytics, see Leandro DalleMule and Thomas H. Davenport, "What's Your Data Strategy?" *Harvard Business Review*, May-June 2017, https://hbr.org/2017/05 /whats-your-data-strategy

10. The GlaxoSmithKline example is drawn with modifications from Thomas H. Davenport and Randy Bean, "Biting the Data Management Bullet at

GlaxoSmithKline," *Forbes*, January 8, 2018, 8/01/08/biting-the-data-management-bullet-at-glaxosmithkline/.

11. The discussion of B2B external data in this section is drawn with modifications from Stephan Kudyba and Thomas H. Davenport, "Machine Learning Can Help B2B Firms Learn More about Their Customers," *Harvard Business Review*, January 19, 2018, https://hbr.org/2018/01/machine-learning-can-help-b2b-firms -learn-more-about-their-customers

Chapter 8

1. Multiple authors, "The Malicious Use of Artificial Intelligence," February 20, 2018, https://maliciousaireport.com/

2. Joel Z. Leibo et al., "Multi-Agent Reinforcement Learning in Sequential Social Dilemmas," Proceedings of the 16th International Conference on Autonomous Agents and Multiagent Systems (AAMAS 2017), ed. S. Das, E. Durfee, K. Larson, M. Winikoff, May 8–12, 2017, São Paulo, Brazil, https://storage.googleapis.com /deepmind-media/papers/multi-agent-rl-in-ssd.pdf

3. Will Oremus and Bill Carey, "Facebook's Offensive Ad Targeting Options Go Far Beyond 'Jew Haters,'" ProPublica, September 14, 2017, http://www.slate .com/blogs/future_tense/2017/09/14/facebook_let_advertisers_target_jew_hat ers_it_doesn_t_end_there.html

4. Scott Shane, "These Are the Ads Russia Bought on Facebook in 2016," *New York Times*, November 1, 2017, https://www.nytimes.com/2017/11/01/us/poli tics/russia-2016-election-facebook.html

5. Edward Moyer, "Facebook's Zuckerberg Speaks Up about Fake-News Fixes," CNET website, November 19, 2016, https://www.cnet.com/news/facebook-mark -zuckerberg-post-fake-news/

6. Kurt Wagner, "Facebook Is Hiring Another 1000 people to Review and Remove Ads," Recode website, October 2, 2017, https://www.recode.net/2017/10/2 /16395342/facebook-mark-zuckerberg-advertising-policies-russia-investigation -election-moderators

7. Mike Isaac, "Facebook Overhauls News Feed to Focus on What Friends and Family Share," *New York Times*, January 11, 2018, https://www.nytimes.com /2018/01/11/technology/facebook-news-feed.html

8. Sheera Frenkel and Sapna Maheshwari, "Facebook to Let Users Rank Credibility of News," *New York Times*, January 19, 2018, https://www.nytimes.com /2018/01/19/technology/facebook-news-feed.html

9. Sheera Frenkel, Nicholas Casey, and Paul Mozur, "In Some Countries, Facebook's Fiddling Has Magnified Fake News," *New York Times*, January 14, 2018, https://www.nytimes.com/2018/01/14/technology/facebook-news-feed -changes.htm

10. Soroush Vosoughi, Deb Roy, and Sinan Aral, "The Spread of True and False News Online," *Science* 359, no. 6380 (March 9, 2018): 1146–1151, http://science .sciencemag.org/content/359/6380/1146

11. Scott Shane and Mike Isaac, "Facebook Says It's Policing Fake Accounts. But They're Still Easy to Spot," *New York Times*, November 3, 2017, https://www .nytimes.com/2017/11/03/technology/facebook-fake-accounts.html

12. For a discussion of algorithmic bias in traditional analytics, see Cathy O'Neil, *Weapons of Math Destruction* (Broadway Books, 2016).

13. Julia Angwin et al., "Machine Bias," ProPublica website, May 23, 2016, https://www.propublica.org/article/machine-bias-risk-assessments-in-criminal -sentencing

14. William Dieterich et al., "COMPAS Risk Scales: Demonstrating Accuracy, Equity, and Predictive Parity" Northpointe Inc. Research Dept., July 8, 2016, http://go.volarisgroup.com/rs/430-MBX-989/images/ProPublica_Commen tary_Final_070616.pdf

15. Ellora Thadaney Israni, "When an Algorithm Helps Send You to Prison," *New York Times*, October 26, 2016, https://www.nytimes.com/2017/10/26/opin ion/algorithm-compas-sentencing-bias.html

16. "Public Safety Assessment," Laura and John Arnold Foundation, http:// www.arnoldfoundation.org/initiative/criminal-justice/crime-prevention/public -safety-assessment/

17. Kaveh Waddell, "How Algorithms Can Bring Down Minorities' Credit Scores," The Atlantic website, December 2, 2016, https://www.theatlantic.com /technology/archive/2016/12/how-algorithms-can-bring-down-minorities -credit-scores/509333/

18. Rachel Botsman, "Big Data Meets Big Brother as China Moves to Rate Its Citizens," *Wired UK*, October 21, 2017, http://www.wired.co.uk/article/chinese -government-social-credit-score-privacy-invasion

19. Michelle Mark, "The Trump Administration's Extreme Vetting Plan Is Being Blasted as a 'Digital Muslim Ban," *Business Insider*, November 18, 2017, http:// www.businessinsider.com/trumps-extreme-vetting-initiative-digital-muslim -ban-2017-11

20. Gideon Mann and Cathy O'Neil, "Hiring Algorithms Are Not Neutral," *Harvard Business Review*, December 9, 2016, https://hbr.org/2016/12/hiring -algorithms-are-not-neutral

21. Josh Constine, "Pyrmetrics Attacks Discrimination in Hiring with AI and Recruiting Games," TechCrunch website, September 20, 2017, https://tech crunch.com/2017/09/20/unbiased-hiring/

22. Ben Lorica, "We Need to Build Machine Learning Tools to Augment Machine Learning Engineers," O'Reilly website, January 11, 2018, https:// www.oreilly.com/ideas/we-need-to-build-machine-learning-tools-to-augment -machine-learning-engineers

23. Gil Press, "Equifax and SAS Leverage AI and Deep Learning to Improve Consumer Access to Credit," *Forbes*, February 20, 2017, https://www.forbes.com /sites/gilpress/2017/02/20/equifax-and-sas-leverage-ai-and-deep-learning-to -improve-consumer-access-to-credit/2/

24. Ron Bodkin and Nadeem Gulzar, "Fighting Financial Fraud with Artificial Intelligence," O'Reilly Conference on Artificial Intelligence, New York, June 28, 2017, https://conferences.oreilly.com/artificial-intelligence/ai-ny-2017/public /schedule/detail/59252

25. Marco Tulio Ribeiro, Sameer Singh, and Carlos Guestrin, "Why Should I Trust You? Explaining the Predictions of Any Classifier," *CM SIGKDD International Conference on Knowledge Discovery and Data Mining (KDD)*, 2016, https:// arxiv.org/pdf/1602.04938v1.pdf

26. Michal Kosinski and Yilun Wang, "Deep Neural Networks Are More Accurate Than Humans at Detecting Sexual Orientation from Facial Images," *Journal of Personality and Social Psychology*, September 2017, https://osf.io/zn79k/

27. Webroot, "Game Changers: AI and Machine Learning in Cybersecurity," December 2017, https://s3-us-west-1.amazonaws.com/webroot-cms-cdn/8115 /1302/6957/Webroot_QTT_Survey_Executive_Summary_December_2017.pdf

28. Kyree Leary, "Experts Warn That AI-Enhanced Cyberattacks Are an Imminent Threat," Futurism.com, August 31, 2017, https://futurism.com/experts -warn-that-ai-enhanced-cyberattacks-are-an-imminent-threat/

29. Maria Korolov, "How AI Can Help You Stay Ahead of Cybersecurity Threats," CSO website, October 19, 2017, https://www.csoonline.com/article /3233951/machine-learning/how-ai-can-help-you-stay-ahead-of-cybersecurity -threats.html

30. George Hill describing a conference speech by Heather Adkins of Google, "The Future of Humans and AI in Cybersecurity," Innovation Enterprise, September 28, 2017, https://channels.theinnovationenterprise.com/articles/the -future-of-humans-and-ai-in-cyber-security

31. Apple Differential Privacy Team, "Learning with Privacy at Scale," December 2017, https://machinelearning.apple.com/2017/12/06/learning-with-privacy-at -scale.html

32. Hiroshi Lockheimer, "Android and Security," Google Mobile Blog, Febru- ary 2, 2012, https://googlemobile.blogspot.com/2012/02/android-and-security .html

33. Ernst & Young survey cited in "Germans Worry Driverless Cars Will Take the Fun out of Their Favorite Pastime," TheLocal.de website, September 19, 2017, https://www.thelocal.de/20170919/car-mad-germany-distrustful-of-driver less-cars

34. Megan Rose Dickey, "Algorithmic Accounability," TechCrunch, April 30, 2017, https://techcrunch.com/2017/04/30/algorithmic-accountability/

35. Ken Krogue, "Artificial Intelligence Is Here to Stay, but Consumer Trust Is a Must for AI in Business," Forbes, September 11, 2017, https://www.forbes.com/sites /kenkrogue/2017/09/11/artificial-intelligence-is-here-to-stay-but-consumer -trust-is-a-must-for-ai-in-business/

36. "Sex, Lies, and AI," SYZYGY Digital Insight Report 2017 (U.S. version), https://think.syzygy.net/ai-report/us

37. Kasey Panetta, "Top Trends in the Gartner Hype Cycle for Emerging Technologies, 2017," Gartner Inc. press release, August 15, 2017, https://www .gartner.com/smarterwithgartner/top-trends-in-the-gartner-hype-cycle-for -emerging-technologies-2017/

38. Jennings Brown, "Why Everyone Is Hating on IBM Watson, Including the People Who Helped Make It," Gizmodo, August 14, 2017, https://www.gizmodo .com.au/2017/08/why-everyone-is-hating-on-watsonincluding-the-people-who -helped-make-it/

39. Russ Mitchell, "Controversy over Tesla 'Autopilot' Name Keeps Growing," Los Angeles Times, July 21, 2016, http://www.latimes.com/business/autos/la-fi -hy-autopilot-controversy-20160721-snap-story.html

40. Discussion from SEB comes from an interview in February 2018 with Erica Lundin and "Burning Passion to Use AI for World-Class Service," press release,

August 21, 2017, https://sebgroup.com/press/news/burning-passion-to-use-ai
-for-world-class-service

41. "Sex, Lies, and AI," SYZYGY Digital Insight Report 2017 (U.S. version), https://think.syzygy.net/ai-report/us

42. Personal email communication from Adam Schneider, January 22, 2018.

43. Deloitte, "Robo Advice Risks in Asset Management," Perspectives document, undated, https://www2.deloitte.com/us/en/pages/risk/articles/robo-adviser
-platform-risks-asset-wealth-management-firms.html

44. Recht is quoted in Ben Lorica, "Building and Deploying Large-Scale Machine Learning Pipelines," O'Reilly website, January 22, 2015, https://www.oreilly
.com/ideas/building-and-deploying-large-scale-machine-learning-pipelines

45. The MIT study is described in Aarian Marshall, "MIT Looks at How Humans Sorta Drive in Sorta Self Driving Cars," *WIRED*, November 20, 2017, https://
www.wired.com/story/mit-humans-semiautonomous-car-study/

46. Nick Carr, *The Glass Cage: Automation and Us* (Norton, 2014).

47. Christopher Mele, "To Improve Your Sense of Direction, Lose the Technology," *New York Times*, January 9. 2017, https://www.nytimes.com/2017/01/09
/science/walking-directions-mobile-phone.html

48. Zoe Fortuijn et al., "Change Management for Watson," IBM Global Business Services White Paper, 2015, https://www-01.ibm.com/common/ssi/cgi-bin
/ssialias?htmlfid=GBW03346USEN

49. Peter S. Goodman, "The Robots Are Coming, and Sweden Is Fine," *New York Times*, December 27, 2017, https://www.nytimes.com/2017/12/27/business/the
-robots-are-coming-and-sweden-is-fine.html

50. Zeynep Ton, *The Good Jobs Strategy* (Amazon Publishing, 2014).

51. Zeynep Ton and Sarah Kalloch, "Transforming Today's Bad Jobs into Tomorrow's Good Jobs," *Harvard Business Review*, June 12, 2017, https://hbr.org
/2017/06/transforming-todays-bad-jobs-into-tomorrows-good-jobs

Index